Railways in Wales

Railways in Wales

Herbert Williams

Christopher Davies
Swansea

Copyright ©Herbert Williams 1981

Published by Christopher Davies (Publishers) Ltd
52 Mansel Street, Swansea SA1 5EL

ISBN 0 7154 0497 0

Composed in 11 on 13 point Garamond, and printed in Wales by Salesbury Press Ltd., Llandybïe, Dyfed

For Peter, David, Alan, Mary and John

Contents

		Page
1	MERTHYR'S ADVENTURERS	11
2	THE IRISH CONNECTION	24
3	BRUNEL'S BROAD GAUGE	41
4	RIVALS IN THE VALLEYS	61
5	THE SUGAR LOAF LINE	80
6	CAMBRIAN CONQUEST	95
7	NARROW-GAUGE PIONEERS	113
8	THE SEVERN TUNNEL	129
9	BARRY'S 'MARAUDERS'	136
10	DISASTER!	143
11	GREAT DAYS OF STEAM	151
12	RAIL REVIVALS	171
13	DIESEL REVOLUTION	184

List of Illustrations

	Page
Richard Trevithick	12
Crawshay Bailey	13
Josiah John Guest	15
Taff Vale Railway contracts	18
Taff Vale time-table	18
Notice to Taff Vale shareholders	18
Early Taff Vale locomotive	22
Thomas Telford	25
Captain Constantine Richard Moorsom	27
Railway navvy, mid 1850s	28
Robert Stephenson	32
Dee Bridge Disaster	34
Victoria at the Britannia Bridge	36-37
The Britannia Bridge	39
Isambard Kingdom Brunel	40
South Wales Railway time-table	43
Railway's appeal for support	44
Trader seeks passengers' patronage	45
Excursion to the Great Exhibition 1851	46
Severn Bridge workmen	48
First train into Swansea, 1850	51
The Landore Viaduct	52-53
Brunel's Chepstow Bridge	55
North Star, Lord of the Isles and Caerphilly Castle locomotives	56-57
Sir Daniel Gooch	59
Punch cartoon — 'The Burial of the Broad Gauge'	60
Broad Gauge engine	63
Vale of Neath iron-bodied coach	64
Vale of Neath rule book	66
Vale of Neath hand signals	67
The Crumlin Viaduct	68-69
Rhymney No. 5 locomotive	72
Rhymney H and I class engine, 1872	75
Brecon and Merthyr engine Hercules	75

Rhymney P class engine 76
Auction of engine 76
M & M locomotive Cader Idris, c.1898 77
Cefn Coed Viaduct 78
Swansea train at Cynghordy 82
Train crossing Cynghordy Viaduct 84
Swansea train climbing the Sugar Loaf 84
Line near Sugar Loaf summit 85
Train at Sugar Loaf tunnel 87
David Davies 89
M & M engine Lady Elizabeth 93
Tailpiece — Rhymney Passenger, engine and coaches 94
David Davies with his spaniel 97
Thomas Savin 98
Sir Watkin Williams-Wynn 100
Benjamin Piercy 101
David Davies at Talerddig cutting 102
Cambrian Railways passenger tender engine 104
Cambrian locomotive Mountaineer 105
Nineteenth century coaches 106
Cashing in on Welsh scenery 106
The Wynnstay locomotive, 1859 107
Cambrian locomotive No. 98 108
Morning express entering Welshpool 109
Montgomery Station 110
Machynlleth Station 110
Festiniog workman's train 111
Trawsfynydd Station 111
Cambrian train at Dolgellau 112
Fairlie's Patent Little Wonder 115
Little Giant 116
Merddin Emrys at Tan-y-Bwlch 117
Ffestiniog viaduct 118
Machynlleth-Corris Railway 120
Corris Station 121
The Welsh Highland Railway 122
Snowdon locomotive Wyddfa 123
The Countess on the Welshpool and Llanfair 124-125
Train at Llanberis 126
Vale of Rheidol engine 127
En route for Devil's Bridge 128
Through the Severn Tunnel into Wales 134
Barry Railway steam coach 138-139
Barry 120 Class K 138-139
Barry passenger tank engine, 1892 141
The Abergele Disaster 144
Aftermath of the Abermule Disaster 149

The Fishguard Express 152-153
The Pembroke Coast Express 154
Denbigh Castle entering Swansea 155
A Capitals United at speed 156
South Wales Pullman headed by a Castle 157
Birmingham-Cardiff rail car, 1934 158
The King George V 160-161
The Red Dragon 162
Western Standard Pacific Rising Star 163
Welsh excursion train at Old Oak 164
Autorail unit at Fishguard 166-167
The Blanche crossing Tanybwlch viaduct 172
L.T.C. Rolt on Talyllyn Railway 175
Railway time-table 176
The Snowdon Mountain Railway 179
Vale of Rheidol tourists 180
Welshpool and Llanfair revival 182
The Fairbourne Railway 183
Inter-City 125 187
Diesel three-car suburban train 188
Diesel-hydraulic locomotive 190
Blue Pullman on London-Swansea run 191
Class 56 diesel-electric locomotive 192
Oystermouth Railway — horsedrawn train 193
Mumbles Railway steam and electric locomotives 194
The Advanced Passenger Train 203

1 Merthyr's Adventurers

O N A FEBRUARY MORNING IN 1804, a curious sight was to be seen in Merthyr Tydfil. A piece of machinery with a tall stack and large wheels stood on the Penydarren tramroad, hissing clouds of steam to the terror of nervous bystanders. For weeks this 'iron horse' had been the talk of the town. It was the invention of Richard Trevithick, a Cornishman who had first come to Merthyr in 1800 at the invitation of the ironmaster Samuel Homfray. Homfray, a born gambler who thought nothing of quaffing a pint and a half of wine before joining a card school, found a kindred spirit in Trevithick. Both were adventurers, eager to challenge orthodox opinions. Trevithick's original task was to build a forge engine at the Penydarren works, but before long he had fired Homfray's imagination with a much bolder idea: the construction of a steam locomotive capable of pulling heavy loads of iron along the tramroad to Navigation (Abercynon), an important point on the Glamorganshire Canal between Merthyr and Cardiff.

Homfray was not a man to do things by halves. He not only told Trevithick to make the locomotive; he wagered £500 on its success. The bet was laid with a rival ironmaster — some say Richard Crawshay of the Cyfarthfa works, others Richard Hill of the Plymouth works. The wager was simply on the engine's ability to travel the nine miles to Navigation with loaded wagons, not on its making the return journey as well. This was fortunate for Homfray, as things went badly wrong on the way back to Merthyr and it had to be ignominiously hauled home by horses. The outward journey, however, was a triumph. With 10 tons of iron in the wagons, plus 70 heroes who clambered aboard without knowing if they were going to live to tell the tale, the contraption puffed laboriously along the tramroad to complete the journey in four hours and five minutes. There were several stops for the removal of rocks and overhanging branches and, more dramatically still, the chimney had to be taken down to allow the train to pass through a low tunnel. The speed was never more than five miles an hour, but history had been made: this was the first time a steam engine had ever pulled a load along a railway.

The *Cambrian* newspaper, published weekly in Swansea, carried a report from a correspondent dated February 22:

'Yesterday the long-expected trial of Mr Trevethick's (sic) new-invented steam-engine, for which he has obtained his Majesty's letters patent, to draw and work carriages of all descriptions on various kinds of roads, as well as for a number of other purposes, took place near this town, and was found to perform to admiration all that was expected from it by its warmest advocates . . . It performed the journey without feeding the boiler or using any water, and will travel with ease at the rate of five miles an hour. It is not doubted but that the number of horses in the kingdom will be very considerably reduced, and the machine, in the hands of the present proprietors, will be made use of in a thousand instances never yet thought of for an engine.'

Richard Trevithick.

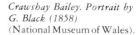

Crawshay Bailey. Portrait by G. Black (1858)
(National Museum of Wales).

Trevithick's locomotive was, however, ahead of its time. It never ran again on the tramroad, and was converted for use in the Penydarren works. For the time being, the horses in the kingdom were safe. Two decades passed before the possibilities of steam transport were exploited, and the laurels then went not to Wales but to the North of England: the Stockton and Darlington Railway opened in 1825, followed by the Liverpool and Manchester in 1830. It was on an autumn day in 1834 that Lady Charlotte Guest, wife of the Merthyr ironmaster Josiah John Guest, wrote in her diary: 'Mr Brunel, of the Thames Tunnel, accompanied by Mr Frere, came here in the evening. They are to make a survey of a railroad from Merthyr to Cardiff, and Merthyr got up soon after six in the morning, in order that he might have a *very* early meeting with them on the subject.' The 'Merthyr' who rose betimes was her husband, to whom she was applying this pet name even before the marriage which her titled family thought disastrous: he was not only twice her age and in trade, but a dissenter too. A dawn meeting was all in the day's work for Isambard Kingdom Brunel, a young engineer who drove himself so hard that he sometimes fell into an exhausted sleep with a lighted cigar in his mouth. At 29 he was already a national celebrity; he had helped his father, Sir Marc Isambard Brunel, construct a tunnel under the Thames, and his plans for a suspension bridge at Clifton had been preferred to those of Telford. Moreover, he had been appointed engineer to the Great Western Railway from London to Bristol, a project that meant far more to him than a mere 'railroad from Merthyr to Cardiff'. Once his advice was sought, however, he gave it with the meticulous care that characterised all his work, and the Taff Vale Railway — which he termed a 'crooked little line down in Wales' — was to be a small jewel in his crown alongside many greater ones.

The need for a railway was self-evident to ironmasters like Guest and Anthony Hill, owners of the Dowlais and Plymouth works respectively, for the difficulties of transporting their products to the coast had become acute. The only artery was the Glamorganshire Canal, which ran the 24 miles from Merthyr to Cardiff, but the world had changed since its triumphant opening in 1794. Quite simply, it could no longer cope with the traffic. In a mere three years the amount of iron carried on the canal had increased by more than half, from 70,333 tons annually to 111,012 tons, and there were long delays. A railway, however, was still a novel idea. There were many who shared the view of the coachmen threatened with redundancy by these 'hissing kettles' that locomotives were against God, nature and the best interests of humanity as well as horseflesh. Some thought their boilers would burst and blow passengers to atoms, and the landed gentry were convinced they would poison the air and polish off the pheasants. Merthyr had its fair share of sceptics, who concluded that since the stage coach to Cardiff barely paid its way a railway was unlikely to do much better. In the words of historian Charles Wilkins, they 'buttoned up their pockets and lived to regret it' when the Taff Vale Railway Company was formed after a meeting at the Castle Inn, Merthyr, in 1835. Brunel, who became involved through his association with the Great Western and his friendship with Hill, estimated the cost as £190,649, and the first advertisement inviting tenders for constructing sections of the line appeared in the spring of 1837. It was the year of Victoria's accession, and when the Taff Vale project was officially launched in August with the laying of the foundation stone of a viaduct at Pontypridd, there were three cheers for the young Queen. 'The Taff Vale railway is now fairly commenced,' observed the *Merthyr Guardian,* 'and we congratulate the proprietors.' It was true that the 'mere lover of the picturesque may lament that a railway, with all its appendages of noise and dirt, smoke and steam, should break in upon the stillness and serenity of nature in one of her most romantic haunts', but these were 'feelings that must yield to the general convenience and public improvement.' Lady Charlotte, whose husband was the chairman of the company, stamped her personality on the occasion by insisting on giving the foundation stone a formal blow not with the 'Lilliputian hammer' that was originally produced but with a wooden mallet, 'to the no small amusement of the workmen.'

Before the first train ran on the line, however, there were some acrimonious quarrels. The directors were accused of mismanagement and in the early part of 1840 Cardiff's MP, Dr Nicholl, said the company's decision to increase its capital by 60 per cent was 'a great injustice to the original shareholders'. The *Railway Times* retorted that he did not seem to know much about the history of other railway companies. The extra cash was needed because of the 'exactions of land owners', which had doubled the cost of land acquisition. 'It would surely be far more grievous and unjust to stop

Josiah John Guest.
(National Museum of Wales).

the work and leave it in an unfinished state,' the magazine declared. Only two months before the opening of the first section of line, the arguments were still continuing. A noisy meeting of shareholders at the Angel Inn, Cardiff, degenerated into farce when the company secretary stood on a chair to read a report and the waiters entered the room while the vote was being taken and laid the table for dinner. A persistent critic of the company who wrote letters to the *Merthyr Guardian* under the nom-de-plume of Fair Play tartly observed that the proceedings were 'the most indecent that ever disgraced a public meeting.' He advised shareholders to 'think and act for yourselves as men. Directors are as liable to err as other people ... No extraordinary capacity is required to comprehend railway affairs. No great mental powers; but merely habits of business.'

Such back-room bickering was of no concern to the brawny 'navigators' who were completing the line. Their legendary thirst was confirmed by a report that eight of them had managed to drink 413 quarts of beer in only 13 days in a Merthyr pub. The track they laid had a gauge of 4ft 8½ in. on the advice of Brunel, who had given his reasons why this 'ordinary width' should be adopted in a letter to the Taff Vale directors dated April 23, 1839. He recommended it 'not as being a peculiarly good width but as being the most commonly used', which had several advantages. 'It must evidently be much easier, that is cheaper, to procure engines and carriages... when all the parts are exactly similar to those always adopted — there is less trouble, there is less risk to the manufacturer.' A 5ft gauge had been proposed, but he argued strongly against it for the same practical reasons. 'An engine of 5ft gauge could not be altered to suit a gauge of 4ft 8½ in. under an expence of £300 to £400, consequently the risks of such an Engine being thrown upon the manufacturers' hands and being unsaleable ... must be covered.' The overriding consideration, however, was the junction with future lines. 'I cannot think that the day is very distant when a direct communication will be made along the coast of South Wales into the interior and thereby to all the great parts of England. The district being embraced by the Taff Vale railway having every profitable facility must by that time have become a manufacturing district to a much greater extent than it now is ... a direct junction between the Taff Vale railway as a branch and such a main trunk would be essential ... All these advantages would be obtained to the fullest possible extent if similarity of gauge permitted a junction — but they would be lost or seriously diminished, if while the difference of gauge prevented a junction with the Taff Vale, other branch lines up the valley of Newport or elsewhere or to the Newport or Cardiff Docks had no such impediment — now this main line will not be a 5ft gauge, it will either be a 4ft 8½ in. gauge or a 7ft gauge — the latter you cannot have and therefore the former offers the only chance.' Brunel went on to explain why, as a zealous advocate of the 7ft broad gauge, which he had persuaded the directors of the GWR to adopt, he felt it unsuitable for the Taff Vale. 'It is hardly necessary to prove that no very great increase can be made in the gauge in this particular case, the natural difficulties of the Country are such as to have rendered unavoidable the adoption of numerous curves of comparatively small radius, and inclined planes — great economy of transport and not speed is the object to be attained . . .' A gauge of 6ft or 7ft, he added, would be 'almost impracticable — certainly very injurious.'

The opening of the first section of track from Cardiff to Navigation House, Abercynon, on October 8, 1840, was hailed as 'a grand day in the ancient town of Cardiff' by the *Merthyr Guardian*. After early frost it was a crisp, clear day, 'and the gay streamers that floated in the breeze, the firing of artillery, and the cheerful strains of music, gave such a holiday air to the scene that it was quite inspiring.' Such festivities always greeted the opening of a railway in those pioneering days and they came as no surprise to Lady Charlotte Guest, who with her husband and other big-wigs from the Merthyr area travelled by train from Navigation House to Cardiff for the official opening. This preliminary journey was not entirely satisfactory. 'We waited some time at the new station house at the Navigation House for the engine to arrive. It had been detained by getting off the Rails in a part of the road only lately laid. In the meantime I enjoyed all the preparations and all the bustle which was going on, — which presented rather a curious scene, the arrangements being anything but complete . . . When the train arrived we took our places in it and proceeded to Cardiff. We had a slight detention on the road owing to the train again getting off the Rails, and we had various stoppages in various parts of the line to take up passengers. We arrived however before twelve, at which hour the great opening train set off and we proceeded again by it back to the place whence we had started . . .' The *Merthyr Guardian* had some barbed comments on the behaviour of the specially-invited passengers who were at last allowed on to the platform for the ceremonial train after the delay mentioned by Lady Charlotte — 'a rush took place, which plainly showed us that the elite of Cardiff are not a whit more polite than the visitors to the pit of the Italian Opera.' As they waited for the train to start they were 'saluted with music and the discharge of cannon' while the vast crowd sent up cheer after cheer. The writer travelled in a 2nd-class carriage, which gave only minimal protection to the passengers, and he remarked on the 'cutting wind' and the 'unpleasant smell of the oil and paint'. The view from the railway, however, was 'infinitely superior to that of the coach road.'

A speed of 25 mph was attained on this initial journey, which showed scant respect for the Parliamentary clause (quickly to be repealed) stipulating a maximum 12 mph on the line. At Navigation House the company 'partook of a luncheon and various kinds of wine, from the sparkling champagne to the humble port.' The braver ladies, led by the redoubtable

Clerk to the Board of Guardians.

TAFF VALE RAILWAY.

Contract for Sleepers.

NOTICE IS HEREBY GIVEN, that the DI-RECTORS WILL MEET at their Office in CAR-DIFF, on WEDNESDAY, the 23rd JANUARY next, to receive TENDERS for the supply of Fifty Thousand Oak, Larch, Beech, or American Red Pine Timber Sleepers.

Specifications of the same and printed forms of Tenders may be had there or at the Engineer's Office, Maendy, near Cardiff, and no others will be attended to.

The Tenders must be delivered at the Office in Cardiff, on or before, 12 o'clock on the said 23rd day of January, and the parties Tendering or parties duly authorized by them must be in attendance at the time of meeting.

The Directors will not bind themselves to accept the lowest Tender.   By order of the Board.
JOSEPH BALL,
Secretary.
Railway Office, Cardiff, December 20, 1838.

TAFF VALE RAILWAY.

Contract for Works.

EXTENSION OF TIME

For Letting the following Contract, from Wednesday the 9th day of January to WEDNESDAY the 23rd day of JANUARY

NOTICE IS HEREBY GIVEN, That the DIRECTORS will MEET at their OFFICE, in CARDIFF, on WEDNESDAY, the 23rd day of JANUARY next, at Twelve o'clock, to RECEIVE TENDERS for the Execution of the following Works, viz.:—

CONTRACT No. 21.

Being the Excavation and Formation of the Cuttings and Embankment, and the Construction of all Bridges, Culverts, and other Masonry Retaining Walls, and the entire Completion (except ballasting and laying the Permanent Rails) of that portion of the Line extending from the termination of Contract No. 15, in the Parish of St. John the Baptist, in Cardiff, to the termination of the Railway in Field marked No. 47 in the Parliamentary Plan, in the Parish of St. Mary, in Cardiff, being a distance of about 85 Chains.

A Draft of the Contract, with Plans and Specifications of the Works, will be ready for inspection at the Engineer's Office, at Maendy, near Cardiff, on and after Wednesday, the 16th day of January next.

Printed Forms of Tender may be had there or at the Office in Cardiff and no others will be attended to.

The Parties whose Tenders are accepted will be required to enter into a Bond with two Sureties for the due performance of their Contract, and the names of the proposed Sureties are to be specified in the Tender.

The Tenders must be delivered at the Office, in Cardiff, on or before Twelve o'clock on the said 23rd day of January, and the Parties Tendering or persons duly authorized by them must be in attendance at the time of Meeting.

The Directors will not bind themselves to accept the Lowest Tender.   By order of the Board,
JOSEPH BALL,
Secretary.
Railway Office, Cardiff, 5th December, 1838.

All work executed on the Premises by experienced Workmen, at the shortest Notice. August, 1850.

TAFF VALE RAILWAY.
ALTERATION OF PASSENGER TRAINS.

ON and after MONDAY, SEPTEMBER 2nd, 1850, the TIMES of DEPARTURE and ARRIVAL of the PASSENGER TRAINS will be as follow, until further Notice:—

UP TRAINS.—WEEK DAYS.

FROM CARDIFF.	H. M.	ARRIVAL AT MERTHYR.	H. M.	ARRIVAL AT ABERDARE.	H. M.
				FROM MERTHYR.... A.M. 8 50	
MAIL .... A.M. 8 40		MAIL .... A.M. 10 0		MAIL .... A.M. 10 0	
P.M. 1 30		P.M. 2 55		P.M. 2 50	
P.M. 5 40		P.M. 7 10		P.M. 7 10	
		SUNDAYS:			
MAIL .... A.M. 9 0		MAIL .... A.M. 10 35		MAIL .... A.M. 10 35	
P.M. 4 0		P.M. 5 35		P.M 5 35	

DOWN TRAINS.—WEEK DAYS.

FROM MERTHYR.	H. M.	FROM ABERDARE.	H. M.	ARRIVAL AT CARDIFF.	H. M.
	A.M. 7 45		A.M. 7 45		A.M. 9 10
		To Merthyr...... A.M. 9 0			
MAIL .... P.M. 1 40		MAIL .... P.M. 1 40		MAIL .... P.M. 3 5
P.M. 5 30		P.M. 5 30		P.M. 6 50
		SUNDAYS:			
	A.M. 9 10		A.M. 9 0		A.M. 10 45
MAIL .... P.M. 4 10		MAIL .... P.M. 4 10		MAIL .... P.M. 5 45

All the Trains leave CARDIFF DOCKS 15 Minutes before leaving CARDIFF, and arrive at CARDIFF DOCKS 10 Minutes after their arrival at CARDIFF STATION.

First, Second, and Third Class Passengers are taken by all the Trains.   For further particulars see the Company's Handbills.

LONDON TIME is kept at all the Stations on this Railway, which is 12½ Minutes earlier than Local Time.   By Order,
Cardiff, August 20th, 1850.   GEORGE FISHER, General Superintendent.

Delivered Carriage Free to all Parts of England.
TEAS AT WHOLESALE PRICES.
TEA WAREHOUSE, 2 BUCKLERSBURY, CHEAPSIDE, LONDON.

THIS Establishment was commenced in the year 1830.   Its SUCCESSFUL PROGRESS during 20 YEARS has gratified our anticipations.   The patronage of the Public has ELEVATED ITS POSITION to one of the LARGEST IN THE TRADE.

TAFF VALE RAILWAY.

Call of Ten Pounds per Share.

THE DIRECTORS of the TAFF VALE RAILWAY COMPANY, acting under the Provisions of the Act of Incorporation, hereby GIVE NOTICE, that the PROPRIETORS of SHARES are requested to pay on or before the 4th day of MAY, 1840, to any of the undermentioned Bankers, the sum of TEN POUNDS, on each of their respective Shares, viz.—

London and Westminster Bank.............*London.*
Messrs. Baillie, Ames, and Co..........*Bristol.*
National and Provincial Bank............*Cardiff.*
Monmouth and Glamorgan ditto...........*ditto.*
Messrs. Wilkins and Co.................*Merthyr.*
By Order of the Board of Directors,
JOSEPH BALL,
Secretary.

Railway Office, Cardiff,
8th April, 1840.

Lady Charlotte, even ventured into the nearby tunnel, which was illuminated for the occasion 'by numerous candles stuck in the sides of the rock', the effect of which she found 'exceedingly striking and picturesque'. Her diary continues: 'The Viaduct looked as beautiful as ever as we issued forth from the tunnel* upon it. We should have lingered longer to examine it but the time was running fast away. So they gave us God Save the Queen and gave three cheers for the Railway &c &c, amongst which was one for me, and then walked back to where the train was waiting ... Anything equal to the brilliancy of the valley I never saw.'

Ironically, the railway was to be instrumental in dulling that brilliancy very shortly, for it initiated great changes which were foreseen that evening in a prophecy which was astute if limited in scope. At a celebration dinner in the Cardiff Arms Hotel, one of the speakers said it would enable farmers to send their produce from the most remote parts of the kingdom into the best markets at a moderate rate. By the aid of steam London was already supplied with beef from Scotland and would shortly, he hoped, be supplied with Welsh mutton. The decision of the Taff Vale directors to run trains on Sundays, however, drew upon their heads the accusation of 'Sabbath desecration'. Only a month after the railway opened, it was reported that a protest had been made by prominent people in the county including magistrates, clergy and some of the 'most respected' shareholders. They declared that this 'violation of the Lord's Day, by the facilities offered by railroads, is deeply felt and deplored by every right-minded person ... as an unmixed evil.' It tempted people to 'leave the peacefulness and solemn duties of their homes and of the day for the sake of pursuing an unprofitable curiosity' or to 'indulge in remote and sequestered spots in irresponsible acts of folly, dissipation and vice.' The directors replied that they were not profiteering but felt they ought to provide the same opportunities for Sunday travel for those who needed it as other railways. They were, however, 'most anxious so to arrange the passage of their trains as not to interfere with the hours of Divine Service.'

There was an early casualty, but the Taff Vale was only indirectly responsible. Daniel Lewis, a Cardiff paper hanger, killed himself with a home-made firework on the day the railway opened. Four days later there was an act of sabotage on the line which could have had far more serious consequences. A train on its way to Newbridge (the early name for Pontypridd) was derailed by a tree trunk placed across the track, apparently deliberately. The directors offered £100 reward for the discovery of the culprit. Half a century later, a writer in the *Western Mail* found the explanation in a 'curious romance'. It had been nothing less, he maintained, than an attempt to kill the driver by a rival for the hand of the girl to whom he was engaged.

Opposite, left:
Two contracts for the taking, as the Taff Vale Railway took shape. The advertisements appeared one above the other in the Glamorgan, Monmouth and Brecon Gazette in January 1839.
(Cardiff Central Library).

Opposite, top right:
The success of the Taff Vale Railway meant readjustments of the time-table from time to time. Note that when this notice appeared in 1850, there was still a difference between 'London time' and local time.
(Cardiff Central Library).

Opposite, bottom right:
A notice which Taff Vale Railway shareholders could not ignore. It was published six months before the first section of track opened between Cardiff and Abercynon (Glamorgan, Monmouth and Brecon Gazette).
(Cardiff Central Library).

---

* At Quakers' Yard, later made into a cutting.

It was the following spring before the line to Merthyr was completed. On the evening of Tuesday, April 20, the bellman went around the town announcing a public holiday next day to celebrate the opening of the full length of railway from Merthyr to Cardiff. People climbed slag-heaps to watch the first train steam out at 8.20 a.m. and the band played 'See the Conquering Hero Comes'. The first four and a half miles were covered in nine minutes 'and at the same rate we continued our comet course through the wild and picturesque defiles of the beautiful Vale of Taff,' to quote a highly-coloured report in the *Merthyr Guardian*. 'Still we flew onward, now skimming o'er the verdant plain, then plunging into the savage ravine, and anon bursting upon the busy haunts of men, who left their labours to gaze upon and cheer us in our passage . . .' There were later trains bringing to Merthyr 'such a number of well dressed and holiday people as we have never beheld before.' It was, in fact, a day 'big with great events for Merthyr — a day for ever memorable as bringing her within an hour of the sea.'

For several months anything to do with the railway was worth a paragraph in the local press. To prove how quick the journey was, a zealous employee of the Taff Vale had his dinner sent up the line from Cardiff to Merthyr. It was reported to have reached him 'having been carefully wrapped up, in as nice a state and as hot as if it had just been cut off the joint', and the experiment was deemed to justify the prophecy that the 'railroad' would 'amalgamate Cardiff and Merthyr so that they would become one place.' Thanks to the Taff Vale, Merthyr housewives were able to buy Bristol veal at 5½ d lb, and in June a train arrived with 70 tons of Lancashire ore after taking only two hours from Cardiff, as opposed to the 17 hours it would have taken on the Glamorganshire Canal.

There were three passenger trains each way every weekday at first, the earliest up train from Cardiff leaving at 8 o'clock in the morning and arriving in Merthyr at 9.25. This had only first class coaches, but the other two 'mixed' trains (which took 20 minutes longer) carried goods as well as second and third class passengers. Third class travel in those days was, by modern standards, horrendous. The passengers were crammed into open vans, known as tubs, which they had to share with livestock and merchandise. The second class passengers were not much better off, for the most they could expect was some kind of covering overhead; the sides of the carriages above waist level were unprotected. Where seating existed at all, it was no more than a wooden bench running around the side of the van. The sheer adventure of railway travel, however, was enough to keep the travellers in good humour, and within weeks the Taff Vale trains were packed with country people going to market with their produce. One day some recalcitrant pigs destined for Pontypridd broke loose on Merthyr station and 'cut away in all directions, nearly upsetting many of the bystanders and causing no little confusion and merriment in the crowd.' There was an innocent delight in happenings which would shortly be regarded as inconsequential, but the promoters took their responsibilities seriously, and were willing to learn: in 1838 they had sent a deputation north 'for the purpose of looking over the Stockton and Darlington Railway and obtaining as much information as possible to enable them to proceed with their large undertaking upon the best system.'

The first engine drivers were imported from north-east England and the locomotives were named *Taff, Rhondda, Merthyr, Cardiff, Llancaiach, Dinas, Dowlais* and *Plymouth*. The *Taff* and *Rhondda*, built in Manchester by Sharp, Roberts and Co., had the distinction of taking the first train to Navigation House in 1840, and they were to give many years of sturdy service to the Taff Vale. The annual report of George Fisher, the company's general superintendent, for 1850 shows how well those early engines had stood up to a decade of hard work. The *Taff, Rhondda* and *Plymouth* were still pulling passenger trains; the *Dinas* was in use on the Llancaiach (Nelson) branch and the *Llancaiach* on the Rhondda branch; the *Cardiff* and *Merthyr* were 'Piloting on Terminus Yard'; only the *Dowlais* had been written off as 'Worn Out'. The company then had 22 engines and Fisher had problems. His report to the directors reads:

'The Rhondda engine has now been running ten years with the same fire box and cannot be called in good condition on that account, instead of the pressure being 70lbs per inch the fire box will not stand more than 50lbs pressure. This engine must have a new fire box shortly and undergo other general repairs and may afterwards last until the year 1853 or 1854. The same may be said of the Plymouth engine. It is true there is very small margin for accidents or contingencies . . .

'Then with reference to Mineral train engines . . . I have bestowed some pains to ascertain the complement allowed upon other lines in proportion to the mileage and I find this Company far under the complement. According to the mileage and effective engines on the London and North Western Railway this Company should have 32 instead of 22 engines . . . The rule adopted here is that each man shall drive but one engine and that the heavy engine shall be out at work three days and in the shed one day, that is with the exception of the engines on the upper end, on the Dinas trains and on the Goods trains, and these I am sorry to say are frequently working for six months without being overhauled further than what is done during the nights . . .'

Fisher recommended buying 'additional mineral engines forthwith' to cope with traffic which had increased from 62,651 tons in 1841 to 711,560 tons in 1849. He thought there were 'reasonable grounds for complaint' that the trains on the line were too heavy, and he was worried about the state of the track. 'I must explain that it could never be contemplated to run large engines at the same velocities as small engines or the effect must be ruinous,'

The Newbridge, one of the first generation of Taff Vale locomotives, built at Bolton in 1846. This is possibly the oldest extant photograph of a railway engine in Britain. Note the railway policemen, with their brass buttons and tall hats.
(South Wales Police Museum).

he contended. Their two latest engines, the *Gadlys* and *Duffryn,* had 17 inch diameter cylinders (those of the *Taff* and *Rhondda* were of 13 inch diameter) and he had issued special instructions limiting their speed to 10 mph. 'I have no hesitation in stating that were the whole of the Company's traffic performed with 17 inch Cylinder engines similar to the two last I should view with serious apprehension their effect upon the permanent way and the probability of accidents . . .'

Seven years later he was still concerned about the state of the permanent way, although much of the original track had been relaid, and he warned: 'Locomotive power will I fear be found an increased item in the Company's accounts: the immense amount of piloting work done at this terminus, the vastly increased number of collieries sending coal to Cardiff, in addition to the quantity now continually sent up the line caused much increased demand for locomotive power; the small engines are now of no use whatever in the coal traffic.'

The faith of the Taff Vale pioneers was thus handsomely vindicated, and the scepticism of those who had seen the iron road to Merthyr leading only to ruin seemed, in retrospect, grotesque. It was hard to credit that, before the black diamonds of the Rhondda and Aberdare valleys began to fill the trucks and the shareholders' pockets, the directors had seriously considered leasing the railway to anyone brave enough to operate it, and that £100 shares had changed hands for only £45. In 16 years the traffic had increased thirty-fold and was approaching 2,000,000 tons annually. 'I do not remember any period,' Fisher reported, 'when the Company had less spare locomotive power than at present.' It was a problem: but one unlikely to disturb the self-satisfied slumbers of the directors of one of the busiest railways, for its size, in the whole kingdom.

2 The Irish Connection

IN THE FIRST DECADE OF THE Taff Vale operation, a much greater enterprise came to fruition in North Wales: the Chester and Holyhead Railway, part of the new line of communication between London and Dublin. It was remarkable for the tubular bridges over the River Conwy and the Menai Strait built by Robert Stephenson, son of George Stephenson, which were the crowning achievements in construction work of immense industry and daring. The Britannia Bridge over the Menai was one of the engineering marvels of its time and thousands travelled in special trains to see it. The Chester to Holyhead line was, in fact, regarded as a national undertaking because of its importance in speeding the mail to Ireland. As the work drew to a close Edward Parry, author of the *Railway Companion from Chester to Holyhead,* was moved to write about it in almost ecstatic prose. At journey's end the traveller would have 'passed through nine tunnels, cut through some of the hardest and most obstinate rock . . . crossed 33 by-roads and four turnpike roads on the level; passed over six public streets, under and over 130 bridges, 15 extensive viaducts and five important tidal and navigable rivers! He will have passed upwards of 100 excavations and embankments; to form which tens of thousands of able-bodied men' have been employed, and *millions* of cubic yards of earth and stone cut and removed!'

The fact is, though, that the railway might not have gone to Holyhead at all. The earliest proposal was that the packets for Ireland should sail from Porthdynllaen, on the north coast of the Lleyn Peninsula near Nefyn, and the claims of Ormeshead (Llandudno) were also advanced. Both Porthdynllaen and Ormeshead, however, were rejected as 'mere roadsteads' by two high-ranking naval officers who emphasised that a Government establishment already existed at Holyhead. The commissioners appointed in 1839 to inquire into alternative routes to Ireland therefore reported that 'the best line of railway for the communication between London and Dublin is that

Thomas Telford — an engraving by William Holl of the engineering genius who first spanned the Menai Strait.
(Photo: P. J. D. Madge).

proposed by Mr George Stephenson, namely, by Chester and Bangor to Holyhead.' Stephenson, designer of the *Rocket,* originally suggested using Telford's suspension bridge over the Menai Strait instead of building a separate one, the idea being to uncouple the locomotive and haul the carriages across by means of ropes attached to stationary engines. John Herapath, a pioneer of railway journalism, was not enamoured of the plan. 'We should not well relish being a passenger in a train going over it in a high wind,' he confessed.

It was 1844 before the bill authorising the railway received royal assent, but by November of the following year 5,000 men were at work. In 1846 the resident director, Captain Constantine Richard Moorsom, gave evidence to the Select Committee on Railway Labourers, an inquiry which typified the stirring social conscience of the times. There were no fewer than 200,000 men employed on railway construction in Britain, and while the committee found the work provided 'steady employment and high wages' the social evils could not be ignored. The men were brought hastily together in large numbers, crowded into unwholesome dwellings, exposed to hard work and great risk to life and limb and often harshly treated. 'Your committee fears that intemperance, disorder and demoralization run a better chance of growth than decency, frugality and improvement and they cannot wonder at the feelings of dislike, and dismay, with which the permanent inhabitants of a neighbourhood often view the arrival of these strangers amongst them,' they reported to Parliament. The men were often paid at intervals of a month or more, and advances were in the form of highly-priced goods from the company store — in other words, the truck system that was later to be made illegal.

The Chester and Holyhead company were good employers by the standards of the day. The men were paid in cash once a fortnight and there was no Sunday work apart from tunnelling, which went on round the clock seven days a week. Captain Moorsom was keen enough on the welfare of railway labourers to suggest that their employers should be required to make periodic returns on the number at work, and to give details of any accidents that had occurred, proposals which the select committee thought should be generally adopted. But his most interesting evidence concerned the company's efforts to improve the moral welfare of their workers. They provided nearly half the cash needed to employ six missionaries to spread the Gospel and entreat the workmen to attend divine worship and send their children to Sunday school. These evangelists, who belonged to the Town Missionary and Scripture Readers' Society, were paid £60 a year to read and talk to the men in their meal breaks, visit their families, distribute tracts and induce those who had some degree of literacy to read improving works for themselves. 'Some of the contractors are decidedly of opinion that the effect has been to keep the men much more steady to their work, and quieter,' said

Captain Moorsom, and another witness maintained that there were labourers on this line who paid between 10d and 1s 6d for Bibles. Astonishingly, he had known some to pay as much as 5s. This represented a considerable sacrifice, since even where labour was scarce a railway navvy could not expect more than 5s for a full day's work, the rate often being only half that. These men were a race apart, not generally given to the kind of respectability remarked on by Captain Moorsom. They descended on quiet country areas like half-tamed savages, content to live in squalid turf huts and going on benders that lasted for days when they had money in their pockets. With the drink inside them they fought like tigers and were regarded as incorrigible corrupters of womanhood. Yet their courage was unquestioned, and

Captain Constantine Richard Moorsom, R.N., — resident director of the Chester and Holyhead Railway during its construction.
(National Maritime Museum).

so was their industry. 'Their powers of endurance were extraordinary,' wrote Samuel Smiles, the apostle of self-help. 'In times of emergency they would work for twelve or even sixteen hours, with only short intervals for meals. The quantity of flesh-meat which they consumed was something enormous; but it was to their bones and muscles what coke is to the locomotive — the means of keeping up the steam... Unburdened, as they usually were, by domestic ties, unsoftened by family affections, and without much moral or religious training, the navvies came to be distinguished by a sort of savage manners... Yet, ignorant and violent though they may be, they were usually good-hearted fellows in the main — frank and open-handed with their comrades, and ready to share their last penny with those in distress.'

Without the aid of mechanical earth-moving equipment, these men performed feats which have been likened to the building of the Pyramids. On the surface they shifted colossal tonnages of soil with pick and shovel, and when driving a tunnel worked deep underground for twelve-hour shifts, soaked to the skin and breathing foul air. They used brains as well as brawn for, wandering from one railway project to another like nomadic tribes, they gained expert knowledge of the peculiar nature of soils and rocks, their contribution to the success of an undertaking being as great as that of the contractors and engineers. The stamina and diligence of the English navvy were legendary. 'Mon Dieu!' exclaimed a Frenchman when he saw these giants of labour bending their backs in the heat of the day, 'how these Englishmen work!' On the Holyhead line the Welsh workmen were less productive at first, but they quickly learned from the example of their comrades. 'They are emulating the English in the extent of work they can do,' Captain Moorsom told the select committee. 'The proportion at the beginning was five Welshmen to three Englishmen in filling wagons, and now they are coming to par.'

By August 1846 there were 12,000 navvies at work on the line, making cuttings, embankments, sea walls, viaducts and bridges, and blasting their way through tunnels with gunpowder. One of the greatest challenges was at Penmaenmawr, where there was no room for a railway between this towering headland and the sea. A terrace was cut out of the rock face and an embankment formed, protected by a sea wall of masonry with a maximum height of 60ft. This was subject to constant assaults by the sea and an October gale caused such extensive damage that part of it was replaced by a viaduct with masonry piers and cast-iron girders. Tough though they were, and often recklessly indifferent to their personal safety, the men could not but be aware of the boulder-strewn mountain looming above them. They were like busy dwarfs beneath a brooding, potentially malignant giant. To protect them from falling stones covered ways were constructed on either side of the tunnel which was driven through the headland, giving it a total length of 453 yards. The works at Penmaenmawr took three years to complete and Robert Stephenson, who had been appointed engineer-in-chief

Railway navvy — artist unknown. Mid-1850s.

after his father's initial surveys of possible routes, admitted that if a longer tunnel had been made in the first instance it would have saved the company between £25,000 and £35,000.

In the meantime, less troublesome sections of the line had been finished. The opening of the 718 yard Penmaenbach tunnel in November 1846 was celebrated in Conwy in style, with flags, banners and music on shore and handsomely decorated ships in the river. In the spring of 1847, however, Robert Stephenson's reputation received a setback when the Dee Bridge he had designed just outside Chester gave way as a train was passing over it, killing five passengers and the fireman. The accident did nothing to convince people that railways were as safe as their promoters held them to be, and the *Chester Courant* reported 'an unprecedented state of excitement and consternation' in the city. Its account goes into graphic detail and shows, incidentally, that the drivers of locomotives were commonly known as 'engineers' at the time:

'When reaching the division of the bridge on the Saltney side of the river, the engineer heard an unusual noise, and felt a kind of vibratory motion in the girders; he immediately accelerated the speed to a great velocity, but had scarcely brought the engine and tender clear over the bridge, when two of the girders gave way, the line of rails on which the train was passing fell, with a tremendous crash, and the carriages were precipitated on to the embankment of the river below, into which some of them rolled... The screams of the slightly wounded, the groans of those whose limbs were broken, and the terror of all, was heartrending... So powerfully wrenching and tremendous was the crash, that the strong iron chains which yoke the train were snapped asunder like bars of glass; and one of the carriages was crushed like a nut-shell by the fall.'

Questions were raised about the design of the bridge but the Chester and Holyhead directors stuck by Stephenson when he staunchly refused to allow a full-time Government inspector on the works at Britannia and Conwy. The official anxiety is easy to understand, since these bridges embodied the revolutionary concept of trains running through long tubes of iron plates connected by rivets. They were, in fact, the only bridges of their kind in the British Isles, and scepticism about their safety was not confined to the general public: the experts themselves were divided. Safety and economy were not the only considerations, however, for the architect Francis Thompson took pains to ensure that the masonry of the Conwy bridge should harmonise with that of the nearby castle.

The first trains crossed the bridge in April 1848 and in May a celebration banquet was held in a pavilion behind the Castle Hotel. It was a sumptuous affair with an interior casing of pink and white calico in alternate stripes, overlaid with evergreens, and toast after toast interspersed with songs from a glee party. Robert Stephenson recalled that when he had first proposed a cast-iron tubular bridge before a Parliamentary committee 'an incredulous glance of the most marked and unmistakeable character was turned upon me by every honourable member.' That glance he could never forget, 'but it did not weaken my conviction.' He proposed the health of Isambard Kingdom Brunel and assured the gathering that between them 'neither difference of opinion nor professional rivalry could engender disrespect.' The quiet appreciation of this magnanimity gave way to amusement when he went on to recall that Brunel had doubted the possibility of floating and lifting the tube, and had advised him to pull his coat off for the chance of a swim across the estuary — 'but his aid in every emergency was never withheld, but always frankly tendered,' concluded Stephenson. Brunel would have enjoyed this, but he had sent apologies for absence. An honoured guest who would not have missed the occasion for anything was George Stephenson, described in the *North Wales Chronicle's* account of the evening as the 'venerable father' of Robert. He was greeted with deafening cheers when he stood to speak, and the master of ceremonies roundly gave 'The health of Mr George Stephenson, with three times three.' Stephenson senior lived just long enough to see his son's own genius confirmed; within a month he was dead.

With the opening of the Conwy Bridge the line to Bangor was complete, and in June an excursion from Bangor to London was advertised 'for 27 Shillings and 6 Pence'! Shortly afterwards cheap summer specials from Bangor offered up to 'sixteen clear days in Town' for fares of £3 first class, £2 5s second and £1 7s 6d third. Meanwhile the still mightier project of the Britannia Bridge across the Menai was going ahead in spite of the company's acute financial problems. Francis Thompson's ebullient design in a combination of Egyptian and Grecian styles embodied colossal lions, 12ft high and weighing 30 tons, carved in limestone on either side of the approaches. Stephenson's original plan was for a bridge of two cast-iron arches, but this was rejected by the Admiralty because they felt it might interfere with shipping. 'I stood, therefore,' he confessed, 'on the verge of a responsibility from which I had nearly shrunk. The construction of a tubular beam of such gigantic dimensions, on a platform elevated and supported by chains at such a height, did at first present itself as a difficulty of a very formidable nature. Reflection, however, satisfied me that the principles upon which the idea was founded were nothing more than an extension of those daily in use in the profession of the engineer.' After assiduous experiments he opted for rectangular tubes, backing the judgement of the engineer William Fairbairn that provided the bridge was well constructed suspension chains would be unnecessary. Nevertheless, the enterprise cost him many hours' sleep. 'Often at night I would lie tossing about, seeking sleep in vain,' he recalled. 'The tubes filled my head. I went to bed with them and got up with them. In the grey of the morning, when I looked across the Square*, it seemed an

---

*By this he meant his home in London — 34 Gloucester Square, Hyde Park.

immense distance across to the houses on the opposite side. It was nearly the same length as the span of my tubular bridge!'

Suddenly this remote part of North Wales became a scene of intense activity. A thousand workmen moved in from all parts of the United Kingdom — skilled artisans, muscular labourers, even 10-year-old lads whose job it was to carry white-hot rivets from the forges with pairs of long pincers. Their panache was such that as they grew in experience they could actually throw their rivets forty feet into the air to the gangs on top of the tubes. A timber platform was erected on the water's edge and the site of the operations covered, in all, no less than three and a half acres. Over 2,000 vessels brought iron plates from Liverpool, Anglesey marble from Penmon and red sandstone from Runcorn in Cheshire. Wagons and carts creaked along the country lanes bringing further supplies, smoke belched from innumerable chimneys, and the roar and clamour of machinery resounded from morning till night. Shops were provided for the workers and their families, and there was even a day school, a Sunday school and a meeting house. The whole operation was a sensation in itself, but in August 1848 there was news of a darker kind with the murder of a watchman — 'one of those fearful deeds of blood,' observed *The Cambrian* luridly, 'which are but too common where large bodies of labouring men congregate.'

Eight lengths of tube were required, their weight being such that at one time the staging supporting them was in danger of collapse and had to be strengthened. By the spring of 1849 work had advanced to a point where a flamboyant gesture was possible—the mounting of a concert in the first tube nearing completion. It was given by the engineering staff of the Chester and Holyhead Railway and the *North Wales Chronicle* tells us that the tube was brilliantly lit for the occasion, with branches at the entrance resembling a grove and seats along the sides for the promenaders. Singers from Caernarfon and Bangor mustered a 40-strong choir and 'all present were struck with the novelty of the thing,' as well they might have been.

Stephenson, however, was not a man to welcome premature celebrations. The greatest task still lay before him — that of floating the tubes from the shore and raising them into position more than 100ft above the waters of the Menai. The floating of the first tube was fixed for Tuesday, June 19, 1849, and metropolitan newspapermen set out to report on an event which had caught the imagination of the entire country. Thousands of tickets were issued to Members of Parliament, peers and other privileged spectators for vantage points overlooking the scene, while lesser mortals gathered on the shore and cliffs. There was a fairground atmosphere, with cake sellers doing a brisk trade and gambling games and travelling amusements on the Caernarvonshire side. The tube, 470ft long and consisting of wrought-iron plates riveted together with thousands of bolts, was an object of wonder and reverence. People stared at it as the Lilliputians stared at

Gulliver. Some even strolled inside it, finding it 'a retreat cool and quiet as a Druids' cave' on such a sultry day, in the words of an imaginative reporter. The day ended in anti-climax with the floating postponed owing to the failure of a capstan, but just as many people turned up the following evening for the second attempt, the traders and professional men of Bangor and Caernarfon having declared a public holiday.

When the tube started on its voyage at 7.30 p.m., about an hour and a half from high water, the shouts of acclaim and wild cheers gave way almost at once to an eerie silence. All eyes were fixed on the great mass floating along the Strait on its pontoons, with Stephenson on top of it directing operations and his old friend and rival Brunel beside him. The band ashore struck up 'I'm afloat' but this jaunty tribute seemed less fitting than the hush that had fallen on the spectators. With a strong tide and high wind the speed of the

Robert Stephenson, the brilliant engineer who took the tubular bridges over the Conwy Estuary and the Menai Strait.
(Science Museum).

tube increased alarmingly and disaster threatened when the guiding cable jammed the capstan on the Anglesey shore, throwing some of the men working it into the water. Charles Rolfe, the foreman, called for help and men, women and children rushed to his aid, grabbing the spare cable and hauling with all their strength. Only thus was the tube brought safely into position, a success signalled by the booming of cannon, the popping of champagne corks and the cheers of the populace. By midnight the tube hung suspended over the Strait with its two ends resting on ledges cut into the rocks at the base of the Anglesey and Britannia towers. It was a 'great event in the annals of mechanics and civil engineering,' reported the *Chester Chronicle,* 'a mingled triumph of science and art.'

Stephenson approached the task of lifting the tube by means of hydraulic machinery with extreme caution, so that four months went by before it reached its final elevation. The floating and raising of the other tubes followed and the men worked day and night to join them together. Meanwhile Stephenson's assistant, Edwin Clark, had been concerned with the permanent way, the rails finally being ordered from the Coalbrookdale Iron Co. At dawn on Tuesday, March 5, 1850 the first train crossed the bridge. It was drawn by three engines, the *Cambrian, St David* and *Pegasus,* bedecked with flags and with Stephenson on the footplate of the leading locomotive. The report in the *Chester Chronicle* indicates that this was regarded as no mere routine but a test fraught with the possibility of catastrophe:

'At precisely 7 o'clock the adventurous convoy, progressing at a speed of seven miles an hour, were lost sight of in the recess of the vast iron corridor. Instead of being driven through with a despatch indicative of a desire on the part of those who manned it to get in and out with the utmost expedition, the locomotives were propelled at a slow and stately pace, with the view of boldly proving by means of a dead weight the calibre of the bridge at every hazard... The locomotives were brought to a stand-still in the centre of each of the great spans, without causing the slightest strain or deflection .... The second experimental convoy that went through consisted of 24 heavily-laden wagons, filled with huge blocks of Brymbo coal, in all, 300 tons. This was drawn deliberately through, at the rate of from 8 to 10 miles an hour, the steam steadily working at quarter power. During the passage of this experimental train through the tube, a breathless silence prevailed that was almost solemn, until the train rushed out exultingly, and with colours flying, on the other side of the tube, when loud acclamations arose, followed at intervals by the rattle of artillery down the Straits... An ordeal stronger still was then resorted to: a train of 200 tons of coals was allowed to rest with all its weight for two hours in the centre of the Caernarvonshire tube, and at the end of the time... it was found to have caused a deflection of only four-tenths of an inch.'

The Britannia Bridge, which cost £674,000 — five times as much as the

The aftermath of one of the earliest disasters. Six people were killed when a girder of Robert Stephenson's Dee Bridge, just outside Chester, gave way in 1847.
(Illustrated London News).

graceful suspension bridge which Telford had thrown over the Menai Strait a quarter of a century earlier — saved the country £60,000 a year by concentrating the packet services at Holyhead. For Robert Stephenson it was simply a job well done, and he coolly refused a knighthood on the grounds that it would be no honour to be ranked with some of those who bore the title. The social effects of the completed line, however, were considerable. The cheapness and convenience of rail travel meant that for the first time day excursions across the border were possible. When a 'pleasure train' of 20 carriages arrived in Chester from Bangor a reporter remarked on 'the singular appearance of the beautiful Caernarvonshire lasses.' It seems that 'their provincial costume, especially their high-crowned broad-rimmed hats, excited particular attention.'

It was by no means one-way traffic, however, and the cheap excursions into Wales made 'staid and stay-at-home English people more familiar with the beauties of North Wales.' Sophisticated travellers found these journeys irritatingly eccentric. At the smaller stations along the Welsh coast the drivers were in the habit of stopping twice, putting down goods at one point and passengers at another. Moreover, 'the guards and servants of the company fetch porter for the passengers, and hob-nob with them in old-fashioned gossip, after the manner of the heavy coaches and their Jehu's of the olden time. This may be all very agreeable to a few jolly fellows and tourists, who are determined to hold facetious company with everybody, and enjoy everything; but it is not quite so suitable for pleasure parties with ladies, who neither smoke, nor chat with the stokers, nor quaff with the jokers, nor take *cwrw da,* or British compounds of malt and Spanish juice, at every village on the line.' For those with social pretensions there were other difficulties. They shunned the Monday excursions because these were popular with the 'lower classes', and a *Chester Chronicle* correspondent seriously suggested running trains in the middle of the week which would be more acceptable to the middle classes.

As well as encouraging closer contact between the Welsh and the English, the Chester and Holyhead Railway initiated the Irish tourist trade. By 1852 monthly tourist tickets were available enabling holidaymakers to travel to Cork and the lakes of Killarney via Bangor, Holyhead and Dublin for fares of £6 10s first class and five guineas second class from London. Seven years later, however, the editors of railway guide-books still found it necessary to emphasise the safety of steam locomotion. The 1859 official guide to the Chester and Holyhead line assured passengers that in the unlikely event of their travelling non-stop by train at a constant rate of 20 m.p.h. it would take them 228 years to be killed in a railway accident. 'Between 1844 and 1851,' the guide declared, 'nearly 7,050 millions of miles were travelled by passengers, of whom 176 were killed from accidents of all causes. Hence only one passenger was killed for over *Forty Millions of Miles* travelled!' The guide also contained 'Hints Before Starting', couched in the language of a schoolmaster patiently instructing none-too-bright pupils:

'Before commencing a journey the traveller should decide (1) Whither he is going; (2) By what railway train, and when; (3) Whether he will have to change carriages at any point, and where.

'The *first* he must settle for himself; the *second* he will learn from Bradshaw, or by consultation with the time-bills of the company, if he will only *patiently* examine them; and the *third* will be readily explained to him if a

*Queen Victoria's visit to the
Britannia Bridge shortly after
it was opened.*
(Illustrated London News).

civil inquiry be addressed to any of the intelligent and obliging guards or stationmasters...

'The traveller is advised to take as little luggage as possible; and ladies are earnestly entreated not to indulge in *more* than seven boxes and five small parcels for the longest journey.

'Do not open the carriage doors yourself; and do not at any station, except those where refreshments are provided, attempt to leave the carriage for any reason whatever, without the knowledge of the conductor, lest you be injured by some accident, or left behind.

'Neither smoking nor dogs are allowed in the carriages; the latter are conveyed under proper arrangements, and at a small charge...

'If part of a journey is to be performed during darkness, we strongly advise the purchase of a railway lamp... The secret of reading in railway carriages... is to prevent the communication of the vibration of the carriages to the arms and book. The elbows should not, therefore, be rested on the solid parts of the carriage, but the book should be held in both hands and supported by muscular power.'

By October 1860 the Irish Mail was leaving Euston at 7.30 a.m. and arriving in Holyhead at 2.05 p.m., which beat the fastest stage coach run of 1836 by fully 20 hours. The 84½ miles between Chester and Holyhead were covered non-stop in new record times of 2 hours 7 minutes down, and 2 hours 5 minutes up. The introduction of sorting offices on the trains and the benefit of a steam-packet crossing from Holyhead to Kingstown (Dun Laoghaire) meant that letters posted in London early in the morning were actually being delivered in Dublin that evening. The average rail speed for the whole journey was 42 m.p.h., and the mail-bag exchange apparatus enabled the mails to be collected and dropped without stopping at fifteen pick-up points. One of the obstacles in the way of this pell-mell progress was the problem of providing enough water for the engines, but this was overcome with the provision of new troughs which replenished the engines while they were still on the run. In 1863 the down Irish Mail was the fastest train out of Euston, and six years later the registration of passengers' luggage was introduced, thus saving them the bother of superintending the transfer of their belongings at Holyhead and Kingstown. Sleeping carriages, with the luxury of a lavatory at either end, made their appearance in the 1870s, and wealthier passengers could buy luncheon baskets at Chester. The 5s basket contained a pint of claret or half a pint of sherry, chicken, ham or tongue, and bread, butter and cheese, while those opting for the 2s 6d basket had to content themselves with a pint of ale or stout, cold meat or pie, and bread and cheese.

There was a close association between the Chester and Holyhead Railway and the London and North Western Railway from the earliest days of the CHR's history. The Chester and Holyhead company ordered their own

engines at first, but even before the completion of the Britannia Bridge they had asked the LNWR to work the line. It was no surprise, therefore, when in 1858 the CHR was vested in the LNWR, which in its turn became part of the London, Midland and Scottish Railway in the sweeping amalgamations of 1922.

The earliest locomotives ordered for use on the Chester to Holyhead line were those of Stephenson's 'long boiler' 4-2-0 type, built by Chas. Tayleur and Co. at Newton-le-Willows. In deference to Welsh sentiment the 2-4-0 engines of 1848 were given names such as *St David, Menai, Conway, Llewellyn* and *Snowdon*. Later came the *Powis, Cambrian, Anglesey* and *Penmaenmawr*, the latter finding itself unexpectedly exiled after five years to the Lancashire and Carlisle Railway. The *Glendower* and *Prince of Wales* made their appearance in 1852, and it should be noted that the directors of the CHR were conscious of the fact that they were operating in a part of the United Kingdom where the first language was Welsh. In 1847 it was agreed that the station staff should be bilingual, and their successors, the LNWR, put bilingual 'Caution' boards at all stations and level crossings west of Mold.

It was a line which took courage to create and constant vigilance against the assaults of the sea to maintain. Pride in its achievements was national as well as local, for it played a significant part in transforming the pace of life and the industrial potential of Britain. In the words of that 1859 guide book: 'The railway system has quickened the pulses of the age . . . Journeys which thirty years ago were measured by days are now accomplished in as many hours . . . without railways, penny postage could not have been carried out, nor the electric telegraph put into operation.' But this was not all. John Bull himself walked with a firmer stride. 'Railways have fortified our coast,' wrote the authors proudly, 'and given force to our national character.'

The Britannia Tubular Bridge, showing the bold combination of Egyptian and Grecian styles.
Pronto Photo History).

3 Brunel's Broad Gauge

THREE MONTHS AFTER THE FIRST TRAIN trundled over the Britannia Bridge, the influential people in the south who had testily observed Stephenson's progress from afar also had something to celebrate. On June 18, 1850, the South Wales Railway was officially opened.

At first it consisted only of 75 miles of double track from Chepstow to Swansea High Street, but great oaks from little acorns grow — and anyone who travels from Paddington to Fishguard today is the inheritor of this initial success. Stage by stage it advanced to bring Brunel's mighty broad gauge locomotives to the route now covered by British Rail's Inter-City expresses. They thundered along a track fully seven feet wide, scaring the wits out of people who had never seen such monsters in their lives before. There must have been many country folk in Wales whose reaction to the first sight of these engines was akin to that of the Wiltshire labourer who remembered the opening of the Great Western Railway to his dying day. 'I heard a roaring in the air,' he told the diarist Kilvert 30 years after the event. 'I looked up and thought there was a storm coming down from Christian Malford roaring in the tops of the trees, only the day was so fine and hot. Well, the roaring came nigher and nigher, then the train shot along and the dust did flee up.'

The broad gauge was used on the South Wales Railway because, from the start, the company was irrevocably linked with the GWR. Its prospectus was issued from the Great Western office in Princes Street, London, in the summer of 1844, with a capital of £2,500,000 in £50 shares. When the formation of the company was announced in the following February the GWR promised to contribute one-fifth of the capital, and its directors confidently stated: 'The other shares of the South Wales Railway have been subscribed for, and there can be no doubt of the Bill being carried, as a great national undertaking to connect the South of Ireland as well as South Wales with the Metropolis.'

Opposite:
Isambard Kingdom Brunel.
(Pronto Photo History).

The Irish connection proved more elusive than it had in North Wales, however, because of lack of funds at a critical time. When at last it was achieved it was by way of Neyland, the original choice of Fishguard having to be set aside for many years. This led to one of the intermittent quarrels between the South Wales and the GWR that plagued their relationship until their amalgamation in 1863 — a union which, however, did not entirely put an end to bad feeling.

The work of constructing the line began in the summer of 1846, but one must not forget the exhausting preliminaries that attended the launching of any railway project. Men such as Brunel and Stephenson had to spend hour after hour giving evidence before Parliamentary committees, enduring the inane questions of the ignorant as well as the caustic cross-examination of the expert. Out of reach of public censure, but with laborious and pains-taking tasks to perform, were the solicitors' clerks cooped up in Dickensian offices, Bob Cratchits who had no redress against the remorseless burning of midnight oil for their masters. Even where thousands of pounds were involved, costs were accounted for down to the last penny. The bill for promoting the South Wales Railway and obtaining Parliamentary approval amounted to £28,923 6s 2d, one of the items of expenditure reading: 'October and November 1844. — 20 Clerks employment upwards of twelve hours every night for 8 days in revising, amending and examining the various copies of the Books of reference to be deposited with the Clerks of the Peace on the 30th Nov. — £241 10s.' Another £2,107 was spent on 'clerks journeys to serve 4,200 notices throughout the line', and the 'use of offices including coals, candles, porter &c and stationery' came to £200. There was a charge of £121 15s for 'fees and gratuities to guides, informants etc', while 'gratuities to doorkeepers of both Houses (of Parliament)' ran up a bill of 10 guineas.

The route west of Newport met with general approval, but in Monmouth-shire there were strenuous objections to the decision to run the line along the coast. It was felt that this would make the county a backwater, and the company was urged to take the railway from Newport up the Usk Valley to Caerleon and Monmouth and hence to Gloucester. This circuitous route was rejected, and another idea that came to nothing was the GWR's initial proposal to avoid Gloucester altogether by crossing the Severn by means of a bridge or tunnel in the region of Awre (between Blakeney and Newnham) at a point where the estuary was only half a mile wide. The Admiralty opposed the plan, and another 40 years were to pass before the much more adventurous Severn Tunnel we know today came into existence. It was thus decided to make Grange Court, near Westbury-on-Severn, the eastern terminus of the South Wales Railway, the remaining eight miles to Gloucester being covered by an arrangement with the Gloucester and Dean Forest Railway Company.

Opposite:
Inter-City travellers today will find a fascination in the original time-table of the South Wales Railway — the broad gauge track which followed the course of the present main line. The company was absorbed by the GWR in the 1860s.
(Cardiff Reference Library).

SOUTH WALES RAILWAY.

ON and after the 19th JUNE, 1850, this Railway will be OPENED for the conveyance of Passengers, Parcels, Carriages, and Horses, between CHEPSTOW, NEWPORT, CARDIFF, NEATH, and intermediate Stations to SWANSEA.—Greenwich time is kept at all the Stations on this Railway, which is Twelve Minutes earlier than Newport and Cardiff time, and Fifteen Minutes before Swansea time.

DOWN TRAINS.

Distance	STARTING FROM	WEEK DAYS. 1st and 2nd, and Parly.	1st and 2nd, Class.	1st and 2nd Class.	1st and 2nd Class.	Sundays only 1st, 2nd, and 3rd Cl.	Sundays only 1st and 2nd, and Parly.
Mls.		a.m.	noon.	p.m.	p.m.	a.m.	p.m.
0	Chepstow	8 0	12 0	4 30	7 0	7 0	6 0
5	Portskewet	8 12	..	..	7 12	7 12	6 12
17	Newport	8 44	12 35	5 5	7 44	7 44	6 44
29	Cardiff	9 15	1 5	5 30	8 15	8 15	7 15
40	Llantrissant, for Cowbridge ...	9 45	1 35	..	8 45	8 45	7 45
49¼	Bridgend	10 15	2 5	6 20	9 15	9 15	8 15
55½	Pyle	10 32	..	..	9 32	9 32	8 32
61½	Port Talbot ...	10 49	2 30	6 45	9 49	9 49	8 49
67	Neath	11 5	2 45	7 0	10 5	10 5	9 5
*	Ticket Platform at Landore						
75	Swansea	11 30	3 15	7 30	10 30	10 30	9 30

UP TRAINS.

distance	STARTING FROM	WEEK DAYS. 1st, 2nd and 3rd Cl.	1st and 2nd Class.	1st and 2nd Class.	1st and 2nd, and Parly.	Sundays only 1st, 2nd and 3rd Cl.	Sundays only 1st and 2nd, and Parly.
Mls.		a.m.	a.m.	p.m.	p.m.	a.m.	p.m.
0	Swansea	7 0	10 30	2 0	6 0	7 0	6 0
*	Ticket Platform at Landore	*	—	—	*	*	*
8	Neath	7 24	10 50	2 24	6 24	7 24	6 24
13½	Port Talbot ...	7 39	11 2	2 39	6 39	7 39	6 39
19½	Pyle	7 52	..	..	6 52	7 52	6 52
25½	Bridgend	8 10	11 32	3 10	7 10	8 10	7 10
35	Llantrissant, for Cowbridge	8 38	12 0	3 38	7 38	8 38	7 38
46	Cardiff	9 8	12 22	4 8	8 8	9 8	8 8
58	Newport	9 40	12 47	4 40	8 40	9 40	8 40
70	Portskewet	10 12	1 12	5 12	9 12	10 12	9 12
75	Chepstow	10 30	1 30	5 30	9 30	10 30	9 30

For the accommodation of the Public, Passengers will be booked by the Up Trains, and put down by the Down Trains marked thus*, at the Landore Ticket Platform, at Fares of 6d., 3d., and 2d. less, according to the Class, than the respective Fare from or to Swansea Station.

COACHES run in connexion with the 7.0 a.m, and 10.30 a.m. Up, and 4.30 p.m. and 7 0 p.m. Down Trains between Chepstow and Gloucester, taking to and from the Great Western Express and other Trains, and with the Trains of the Midland Railway Company, from Gloucester to the North of England; Coaches will also run between Chepstow and Bristol via the Aust Passage, from the 7, 10, 30, and 2 Up Trains, and will also work from Bristol to the 8, 4.30, and 7 Down Trains; but while every exertion will be made to ensure punctuality, this Company cannot be responsible for any delay or inconvenience which may arise from any detention of the Coaches or Trains. Coaches also leave Chepstow, Newport, and other Towns, for Hereford, Pontypool, Abergavenny, and also from Swansea for Carmarthen, Tenby and Haverfordwest, &c.; information respecting which may be obtained at any of the Company's Stations.

STEAM BOATS, between Bristol and Chepstow, ply daily, on the arrival of certain Trains, depending on the state of the tides, particulars of which can be ascertained at the Stations.

FARES.

DOWN.

FROM CHEPSTOW TO	1st Class.	2nd Class.	3rd Class.	CARRIAGES. 4wheel	CARRIAGES. 2wheel	HORSES. Each.	HORSES. Per pair, being the same property.
	s. d.	s. d.	s. d.	s. d.	s. d.	s. d.	s. d.
Portskewet	1 0	0 9	0 5	..	..	..	..
Newport	3 6	2 6	2 0	15 0	10 0	10 0	16 0
Cardiff	6 0	4 0	2 5	18 0	13 0	14 0	21 0
Llantrissant	8 0	5 6	3 4	25 0	18 0	20 0	29 0
Bridgend	10 0	7 0	4 1	29 0	21 0	23 0	34 0
Pyle	11 0	7 9	4 7	..	..	..	..
Port Talbot	12 0	8 6	5 1	34 0	25 0	27 0	40 0
Neath	13 6	9 0	5 7	36 0	26 0	29 0	43 0
Ticket Platform at Landore	14 6	9 6	6 1	..	..	..	..
Swansea	15 0	10 0	6 3	40 0	28 0	31 0	47 0

UP.

FROM SWANSEA TO	1st Class.	2nd Class.	3rd Class.	CARRIAGES. 4wheel	CARRIAGES. 2wheel	HORSES. Each.	HORSES. Per pair, being the same property.
	s. d.	s. d.	s. d.	s. d.	s. d.	s. d.	s. d.
Neath	1 6	1 0	0 8	8 0	6 0	7 0	12 0
Port Talbot	3 0	1 9	1 1	10 0	8 0	9 0	13 0
Pyle	4 0	2 6	1 7	..	..	..	..
Bridgend	5 0	3 0	2 2	19 0	14 0	15 0	22 0
Llantrissant	7 0	4 6	3 0	23 0	17 0	18 0	27 0
Cardiff	9 0	6 0	3 10	28 0	20 0	22 0	32 0
Newport	11 6	7 6	4 10	33 0	23 0	26 0	38 0
Portskewet	14 0	9 6	5 10	..	..	..	..
Chepstow	15 0	10 0	6 3	40 0	28 0	31 0	47 0

REGULATIONS.

FARES FOR DOGS each.—For a distance not exceeding 20 miles, 6d.; 50 miles, 1s.; above 50 miles, 1s. 6d.

DAY TICKETS at a reduction of One-fourth of the Double Fare, and available for the same day, will be issued to First and Second Class Passengers. The Return Journey may be made with Day Tickets by any Train which leaves the Station before 12 o'clock on the same night, even if it does not arrive at its destination within that time. Saturday Tickets will be returnable on the day they are issued, or on the following Sunday or Monday. Sunday Tickets, in like manner, will be returnable on the day they are issued or on the Monday following. Passengers desirous of stopping on their journey are requested to take their Ticket to such Station only. Day Tickets cannot be used to proceed by a later Train beyond the Station at which the Passenger may first alight. In all cases, there are, fresh Tickets must be taken to proceed by any subsequent Train.

The published Train Bills of this Company are only intended to fix the time at which Passengers may be certain to obtain their Tickets for any journey from the various Stations, it being understood that the Trains will not start from them before the appointed time. Every attention shall be paid to ensure punctuality, as far as it is practicable; but the Directors give Notice, that the Company do not undertake that the Trains shall start or arrive at the time specified in the Bills; nor will they be accountable for any loss, inconvenience, or injury, which may arise from delays or detention. Passengers booking at intermediate Stations can only do so conditionally, upon there being room in the Train.

CARRIAGES and HORSES, being at those Stations which are distinguished by Black Letter Type 10 minutes before the specified time for the departure of the Trains, will be conveyed on this Railway.

A GROOM in charge of four or more Horses will be entitled to a Free Pass.

PASSENGERS IN PRIVATE CARRIAGES (not being Servants) are required to take First-class Tickets, as the Carriage rates do not allow for reduced Fares, and such Passengers may change on the Journey to the Company's First-class Carriages if they please.

CHILDREN under Three years of age travel free; and those above Three and under Twelve, at Half-price.

LUGGAGE.—First Class Passengers are allowed 112 lbs. of Luggage, and Second and Third Class Passengers 56 lbs. of Luggage, free of charge; all excess will be charged for according to distance. Passengers are requested to see the Company's labels placed on each article of their Luggage. In order to prevent delay and inconvenience on the re-delivery of Luggage at the end of the journey, Passengers are requested to place on each article their name and address. And notice is hereby given, that the Company will not be responsible for the care of the same unless booked and paid for accordingly.

PARCELS may be booked at any of the Company's Stations for conveyance to the different Stations on the Line, and to Bristol, Gloucester, Cheltenham, and all Stations on the Great Western Railway and Midland Railway, and for Carmarthen, Towns and Villages adjacent to the South Wales Railway, and for Carmarthen, Tenby, Haverfordwest, &c. &c. &c.

POST HORSES can be obtained at the principal Stations on this Railway on the arrival of the Trains.

GLAMORGANSHIRE CANAL NAVIGATION. | The Present Proprietor of HALSE'S CELEBRATED

A slump in the fortunes of railways all over Britain in the latter part of the decade led to the temporary abandonment of the works in Carmarthenshire and Pembrokeshire, so for the time being the directors narrowed their sights to take in Swansea on the one hand and Chepstow on the other. This gave them quite enough to think about, for the engineering works involved large timber viaducts at Landore and Newport as well as the Newport tunnel. The going was made even rougher by a fire which destroyed the 1,200ft Newport viaduct over the Usk on May 31, 1848. A hot bolt being driven into the middle truss started the blaze, and a high easterly wind fanned the flames to make an inferno far beyond the resources of the town's lumbering old fire engine to combat. For the people of the town it was a spectacle not to be missed, and a jostling crowd on the nearby stone bridge saw the middle of the viaduct fall in a huge mass as darkness fell. 'The bridge has been nearly two years in construction,' observed the *Cardiff and Merthyr Guardian* plaintively, 'and in about four hours almost the whole of it was destroyed.' When it was renewed, Brunel substituted wrought-iron bow-string girders for timber in the centre span.

As the year progressed, the appearance of hordes of navvies aroused the usual mixture of fear and excitement among the local population. 'More than 120 railway excavators reached Cardiff by steamer from Bristol on Tuesday and proceeded westward', the local press reported in September. One of them was killed at St Fagans in October by a fall of earth, and a fortnight later several of those working on the other side of Cardiff applied for a summons against their ganger on the grounds that he was not paying them their due amount. 'We are obliged to get up at 4 o'clock in the morning to get ready for our work,' one of the plaintiffs told the Cardiff magistrates, 'and then we go and work in the wet thinking we shall get a little money, and it's too bad to think we shan't be paid at all.' Their case aroused some sympathy, the magistrates speaking kindly to them but pointing out that

Three months after the opening of the South Wales Railway from Chepstow to Swansea, an enterprising tradesman made this direct bid for the patronage of its passengers (Cardiff and Merthyr Guardian). (Cardiff Central Library).

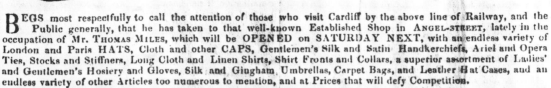

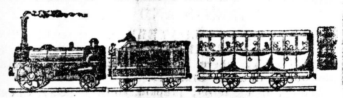

SOUTH WALES RAILWAY.

—

GREAT EXHIBITION OF ALL NATIONS.

—

AN EXCURSION TRAIN

WILL Start from SWANSEA for LONDON at 5 A.M., on MONDAY, the 1st SEPTEMBER, viâ NEWPORT, by the SCREW STEAM PACKET CO., to BRISTOL, thence by SPECIAL TRAIN on the Great Western Railway; and will return to SWANSEA from PADDINGTON on MONDAY, September 8th, at 11 A.M.

TIME AND FARE TABLE, INCLUDING PACKET FARE.

	Starting at a. m.	1st Class. s. d.	Covered Carriages s. d.
Swansea to London & back	5 0	23 0	17 0
Neath, calling at	5 20	22 0	16 6
Port Talbot	5 35	21 6	16 0
Bridgend	6 5	20 6	15 6
Llantrissent	6 33	20 0	15 0
Cardiff	7 0	19 0	14 0
Newport	7 30	16 6	12 6
Chepstow for Newport, by 7.15 Down Train	7 15	19 6	14 6

The Trains are so arranged, that no detention beyond that necessary for the embarkation of the Passengers will arise at Newport or Bristol, on account of the Tides.

No Luggage exceeding a Trunk, Portmanteau, or Carpet Bag, will be allowed to each Passenger.

The Tickets will only be available for the Trains and Dates above named. Passengers not returning by the Special Trains, will lose the advantage of the Return Journey, except at the ordinary fares.

In order to provide the necessary accommodation, no Tickets will, under any circumstances, be issued at any of the South Wales Stations after 7 P.M. on SATURDAY, the 30th August.

☞ Passengers desirous of visiting SLOUGH and WINDSOR, will be able to do so by Special Trains, on the Great Western Railway, on Sunday Morning.

FARES —Paddington to Windsor and back, 2s. each.

From the start, railway directors were alert to the possibilities of excursion trains. The Great Exhibition of 1851 inspired this special offer (Cardiff and Merthyr Guardian).
(Cardiff Central Library).

since they were employed east of the Rhymney river they would have to apply to a Monmouthshire court.

The deeds and misdeeds of the navvies frequently made the densely-packed pages of the *Cardiff and Merthyr Guardian*. A drunken argument between husband and wife which resulted in the unfortunate woman climbing a wall and throwing herself into waist-deep water the other side was regarded with amusement, newspaper scribes of that time tending to take a patronising attitude towards the lower classes. An assault on a Cardiff constable met with a 10s fine and a clacking of tongues in respectable circles, and the murder of a local man in the notorious Stanley Street area provoked, not surprisingly, 'a great outcry'.

There was happier news just before Christmas when the broad-gauge locomotive *The Dove* reached Tidenham for the cuttings near Mead's House. It had been hauled from Gloucester on a specially-built carriage drawn by 18 fine grey horses, with four black horses pulling the tender. Shortly afterwards *The Phantom* arrived in Bute Docks to be placed on a massive wagon with the aid of machinery and drawn through Cardiff by a team of 18 horses 'amidst the admiring gaze of large numbers'. The making of the railway was, in effect, a continual public entertainment. 'One of the most pleasing prospects from St Mary's Street in this town,' observed a Cardiff reporter in January 1849, 'is that of the men at work across the moors in forming the line of this railway.' Winter rains held up the operation from time to time, and when the Taff and Ely overflowed their banks to bring knee-deep water swirling through the village of Canton, the railway works in the vicinity were flooded.

With the coming of spring the tempo quickened, and in April Brunel was said to have 'minutely inspected' the works around Cardiff, Bridgend and Neath. He urged the contractors to be diligent and 'seemed satisfied'. By now there was a local man at the helm — C. R. M. Talbot of Margam Park, Lord Lieutenant of Glamorgan, who had become chairman of the company in succession to Charles Russell of the GWR. The *Cardiff and Merthyr Guardian* approved the change, which came during the frantic period of speculation known as the Railway Mania. The paper gravely observed that at a time when the 'reckless proceeding of some of the heads of our great railways have tended to bring railway speculation into very great discredit', and the public were being lured into buying shares by hollow promises, the appointment was doubly acceptable.

In Cardiff the construction of the railway brought a major change in the face of the town, the course of the Taff being altered so that it no longer took an easterly curve from Cardiff Bridge but ran straight towards Penarth. This had far-reaching consequences, for it enabled Westgate Street to be built in the latter part of the century, and — an event of much greater magnitude — the creation of the Welsh rugby mecca of Cardiff Arms Park. The immediate

Some of the men who built the Severn Bridge in the 1870s.
(British Railways).

effect, however, was to threaten the Batchelor brothers with ruin. They had a shipbuilding yard near the Golate, the alley which ran from St Mary Street to a quay on the river, but the diversion of the Taff made it useless and they demanded compensation. They had a sound case, but some landowners in the Vale of Glamorgan were simply out to milk the railway company. Sir Thomas Digby Aubrey, for instance, turned down an offer of £2,200 compensation, claiming £4,134. He went to law and came out much the worse for it, with an award of only £2,110. Brunel was infuriated by the obstinacy of the local landowners, complaining that the task of obtaining possession of land had been greater on the South Wales line than any other he had known.

The news that the railway was to be officially opened on June 18 — a significant date in the calendar then, as it was still being celebrated as

Waterloo Day — did not reach Cardiff until two days beforehand, which happened to be a Sunday. It was received with great excitement, the sober nature of a Victorian Sabbath being seriously undermined as people ran into the streets and practically mobbed anyone lucky enough to have a time-bill (time-table) in his possession. The ceremonial run on Waterloo Day was described in great detail in the *Cardiff and Merthyr Guardian,* which found virtue even in the unyielding ugliness of some of the stations:

'We are by no means advocates of lavish expenditure and gaudy show, on buildings designed for active everyday business; and, looking narrowly at the Chepstow station, we cannot say that a single farthing has been expended unwisely, so far as appearance, convenience and extent are involved. The station, goods shed, carriage shed, and other offices, are all constructed upon the most economical but nevertheless the most useful principles.'

In his enthusiasm the writer of this eulogistic report even attempted a description of the sound the train made as it started its journey: 'Phou! phou! phou! sche! sche! sche!' Wherever the train stopped there was a party of local dignitaries waiting to hand a congratulatory address to the directors, and at Cardiff they toasted the success of the venture in champagne. Adventurous lads clambered on to roof tops near the station to watch the train arrive in style, its two engines decked out with evergreens. It passed beneath a huge banner bearing the words, 'Success to the South Wales Railway and the trade of Cardiff', and one of the directors was so impressed with the smart turn-out of the local constabulary that he sought out the sergeant to compliment him. At Bridgend a band was on the streets four hours before the train was due to arrive, and the Rev. Robert Knight, of Tythegstone Court, was handed a letter signed by leading citizens thanking him for his exertions in helping to bring the railway to the town. This attitude contrasted with that of the people of Cowbridge, who decided they did not want it anywhere near them and lived to regret it as trade slumped with the extinction of stage coach travel.

The train, with plush saloon cars for the directors and their ladies and open carriages for the less exalted, reached journey's end at Swansea after passing through triumphal arches galore and being greeted by the roaring of cannon, the fluttering of flags and the pealing of church bells along the route. The crowd at Swansea station was such that it was impossible to move against the tide, and Brunel was given the kind of rapt attention that later generations were to reserve for figures other than railway engineers. He was, according to one report, 'gazed at and viewed most unmercifully — all having heard of him, but few having had opportunities of seeing him'.

Brunel, biting the inevitable cigar, fumed at the delay. Public adulation meant little to him: the work itself was everything. At the banquet held that afternoon in a marquee in Burrows Square, he let others do the talking. Talbot looked forward to the expansion of the railway to Carmarthen and

Pembroke, 'so that the whole of South Wales and Monmouthshire might be united as one nation', and the mayor of Swansea, Christopher James, recalled the scepticism of those who, only a decade ago, had seen no future in railways. The promoters of the Taff Vale had been told by these Jeremiahs that their receipts from passenger traffic would not exceed £1,000 annually, 'but for the first year the revenue was £17,392'. The company murmured its approval, replete not only with the satisfaction of those enjoying the sensation of being wise after the event but with the repast to which they had done full justice. They had tucked into a feast of Pickwickian proportions, itemised by an assiduous reporter thus: 'eight hams, 19 dishes lamb, six ditto roof beef, nine ditto veal, four ditto collared veal, three fore-qtrs lamb, three collared heads, 45 couples fowls, 12 raised pies, 12 chicken ditto, eight forced fowls and jelly, 30 large lobsters, seven ditto crabs, 40 lobster, crab, Italian, and other dishes, 70 moulds jellies &c, 12 fruit tarts, 30 dishes of pastry, 35 large cakes, consisting of savoy, almond and pound, some of which were ingeniously ornamented with railway devices &c'.

The *Cardiff and Merthyr Guardian*, while faithfully recording such culinary detail, also found space for a little sermon on the social value of railways:

'One of the minor but still important features of the introduction of the railway system will be the facilities which it will afford for the formation of excursion parties to visit the different localities that are distinguished by the beauty of their natural scenery . . . In this point of view, railways are essentially *democratic* in every nobler sense of the term, for they enable, by combination of numbers, the mechanic and the labouring man from the crowded town or alley to enjoy the rich feast at nature's board which has hitherto been the almost exclusive social privilege and distinction of the wealthier classes . . .

'In the midland and northern districts of England, the mechanics have widely availed themselves of the penny-a-mile trains for this purpose, and we trust to see their example extensively followed by the same classes in Wales . . . Depend upon it, that of the two or three thousand men who join in these pleasure trips, there is scarcely one who does not return a wiser and better man.'

The line opened for general traffic the day after the ceremonial run, with four trains daily in each direction on week-days and two on Sundays. The fastest were the 4.30 p.m. Chepstow-Swansea and the 10.30 a.m. Swansea-Chepstow, both of which took three hours for the journey carrying first and second class passengers only. The first train of the day out of Chepstow left at 8 a.m. to arrive in Newport at 8.44, Cardiff at 9.15, Bridgend at 10.15, Port Talbot at 10.49, Neath at 11.05 and Swansea at 11.30. It was a 'Parliamentary' train, so called because it complied with Gladstone's Act of 1844 stipulating that every railway company must run at least one train a day

First train into Swansea in 1850.

providing third class passengers with seats and covered accommodation at fares not exceeding a penny a mile. The first class carriages of the time were modelled on the old stage coaches, even to the extent of having luggage on the roof and a guard seated there to look after it! Passengers were allowed to take their own private carriages on the train, paying first class fares and with the opportunity to transfer to one of the company's first class carriages during the journey. A groom in charge of four or more horses was entitled to a free pass. The fare from Chepstow to Swansea was 15s first class, 10s second and 6s 3d third, and day tickets (day returns) reducing the double fare by a quarter were available to first and second class passengers.

It was not the custom to travel light in those days, a fact made clear by the generous limits allowed passengers in the amount of luggage they could carry free. For first class passengers this was no less than 112 lbs, with the others being allowed half that amount. The warning that 'Greenwich time is kept at all stations' reminds us that in 1850, the time of day depended on where you were. When it was 8 o'clock in London it was 8.12 in Cardiff and 8.15 in Swansea, a complication which hastened the adoption of Greenwich time throughout Britain. The company's time-table looks straightforward enough at first glance, but an examination of the small print reveals this qualification: 'The published Train Bills of this Company are only intended

One of Brunel's greatest works in Wales — the Landore Viaduct.
(Illustrated London News).

to fix the time at which Passengers may be certain to obtain their Tickets for any journey from the various Stations, it being understood that the Trains will not start from them *before* the appointed time.' Travellers were assured that every effort would be made to ensure punctuality, but the directors gave notice 'that the Company do not undertake that the Trains shall start or arrive at the time specified in the Bills,' which must be viewed not as an indication of indifference but as an honest admission of fallibility.

Passengers with an eye for engineering skill had much to admire along the route. There was the Landore viaduct over the Tawe and its marshes, one-third of a mile long with 37 spans varying from 40 ft to 100 ft. The piers were

of different materials, some almost entirely of masonry, some combining masonry with timber, and others made entirely of timber. Brunel, in constructing it, drew on the experience he had gained in the West of England: the South Devon Railway, skirting Dartmoor, crossed four deep valleys by lofty viaducts all of the same design. There were serious problems at Llansamlet, where frequent landslips threatened a deep cutting through the coal measures. Brunel's answer was a perfect example of his inventive genius, for he made use of the principle of the 'flying bridge', first employed in cuttings on the Bristol and Exeter Railway. This had a single arch reaching from one side of the cutting to the other and springing from the slopes, which it helped to support. At Llansamlet he threw four flying arches across the cutting at short intervals and weighted them with heavy copper slag, so that the sides of the cutting were made secure by the thrust of the loaded arches.

At Chepstow, however, a much greater challenge awaited him. The River Wye had to be crossed at a point where the east and west banks were radically different: to the east a sheer limestone cliff rose to a height of 120 ft above the river bed, but on the opposite bank the land sloped gently for a considerable distance only a few feet above high water. Brunel achieved the 50 ft minimum clearance required for shipping in these tidal waters by making a high embankment to the west and cutting into the cliff about 20 ft below the top. The 600 ft bridge he constructed had a river span of 300 ft and three land spans of 100 ft each, supported on piers made out of cast-iron cylinders filled with concrete. The task of driving these cylinders through the soft boulder clay and marl to reach solid rock 30 ft beneath the river bed and 84 ft below high water is yet another tale of ingenious Victorian engineering and herculean labours. After sealing the top of a cylinder, air was pumped in to expel the water at the bottom. Workmen then entered it through an air lock to excavate the ground, and weights were added to the cylinder to make it sink. When time ran short, the pneumatic method of sinking which Brunel's father, Sir Marc Isambard Brunel, had used at Rotherhithe was also employed.

Working two or three at a time inside these cylinders, which varied between six and eight feet in diameter, the men had to fight back fears of being drowned or buried alive. A 30 h.p. engine pumped out the fresh water which came rushing in, and sometimes huge volumes of soft river silt would burst in with such force that they barely had time to escape. The *Railway Times* meticulously detailed the geological strata, stating that the men had dug through nearly 29 ft of blue clay and sand, a thin bed of peat, four feet of fine blue gravel, a bed of boulders and a bed of red marl five feet thick before reaching the solid rock known as millstone grit.

The central span across the river made use of the suspension principle. The roadway girders were carried on suspension chains hung from horizontal circular tubes which rested on piers rising about 50 ft above the level of the rails.* The floating of the tubes was like a repeat performance in miniature of the Britannia operation. Brunel attached strong cables to moorings to counteract the rapidity of the tide, and the pontoons were under the capable control of Capt. Claxton R.N., an experienced hand in these matters. The opening of the 'Great Railway Bridge at Chepstow' in July 1852 was greeted by the *Monmouthshire Merlin* as 'the auspicious day, so long desired by railway shareholders, men of business, and tourists, when an

---

* The bridge today is fundamentally different from Brunel's conception. The land spans were replaced in 1949 and the central span and tubes were removed in 1962 and replaced with underslung girders. The original piers, however, and Brunel's south-west abutment still remain.

unbroken line of railway should connect South Wales with the Metropolis of the Empire.' Its report continued:

'Glorious sunshine . . . welcomed the event; cannon roared and reverberated from rock to rock upon either bank of the beautiful Wye; St Mary's mellow-toned bells rang inspiring peals; music filled the air; gay flags waved from many a height; the public were determined to devote to pleasure a day on which so magnificent a triumph of engineering skill, and so fine a feature of their neighbourhood, was open.'

When it came to describing the test run over the bridge, the reporter's excitement was such that he actually called the great engineer 'the Brunel', as if he were some mythological creature:

'At twenty minutes past eleven o'clock, the note of preparation was sounded. The Stentor locomotive (decorated with the national flag and laurels) placed temporarily in the hands of Mr Marteley, the superintendent of the locomotive department, accompanied by Pickering, engine driver, came forth, fuming as if eager for the honour of winning the pass. The Brunel was there, with keen eye and the judgement of a master mind, to perform the crowning act of this stupendous undertaking. The Napoleon of Railways stood upon the Stentor, about to pass as a victorious chieftain on conquered ground, the way won by his genius over gigantic obstacles. There he stood, looking upon the great work of his brain, with a calm countenance . . . indifferent of all spectators.'

After the train had safely crossed the bridge, 'some gentlemen who had nervously inclined to suppose that the passage could never be made in safety,

The physical growth of the railway engine graphically illustrated — the broad gauge North Star (1837) is dwarfed by the Caerphilly Castle (1923). The Lord of the Isles (centre) was built in 1851. (Pronto Photo History).

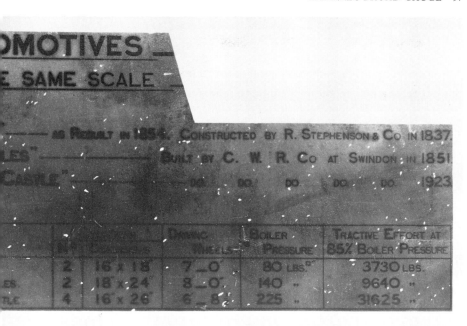

OMOTIVES

E SAME SCALE

——— as Rebuilt in 1854. Constructed by R. Stephenson & Co in 1837.

LES" ——— Built by C. W. R. Co at Swindon in 1851.

Castle" ——— do.   do.   do.   do.   do.   1923.

N°	Cylinders	Driving Wheels	Boiler Pressure	Tractive Effort at 85% Boiler Pressure
2	16 × 18	7 – 0	80 LBS.	3730 LBS.
2	18 × 24	8 – 0	140 "	9640 "
4	16 × 26	6 – 8	225 "	31625 "

were now satisfied that all was right, and desired to be received into the company of the adventurers on their return passage.'

Now that through traffic from London to Swansea was possible, the GWR's 999-year lease of the South Wales Railway came into operation. The line was managed by a joint committee of five directors from each company, with the Great Western providing engines and rolling stock and the South Wales Railway accommodation for the traffic. The staff, other than the locomotive department, remained employees of the South Wales Railway.

Later that year the 30-mile extension of the line from Landore to Carmarthen was completed. It had been hoped to have this ready before September was out, but a Government inspector ruled that part of it needed attention. The news of the delay did not filter through in time to stop dozens of people from Pembrokeshire and Cardiganshire travelling by stage coach to Carmarthen in the hope of going by train to England. Extra coaches were put on the road to take them to Swansea.

The line was eventually opened on October 11, 1852, and met with immediate success. 'It is really astonishing what large numbers of people have during the week travelled over the line,' observed the *Carmarthen Journal.* 'Omnibuses, cabs &c are rattling away through the streets to the station from an early hour in the morning until late at night. This has imparted an unwonted bustle and excitement to the town.' A week later the paper reported that on the previous Sunday over 300 people from Llanelli, Swansea and Merthyr had visited Carmarthen 'and an equally large number of tradesmen and mechanics took an excursion to Swansea by the train.' On October 29 the editor ran a leading article stating:

Wales is growing in importance. A few years ago, the Principality was an isolated and unknown country. Its language and mountains formed an impassible (sic) barrier to the enterprising Englishman . . . Through the inherent energy of the Welsh, and their untiring perseverance, Wales is now attaining a high position, and sending forth its treasures in rich abundance. The Principality has its "hives of industry", and its commercial marts. Every year increases the number. Now that the railroad pierces the country, they will speedily multiply. The future is most promising. Let us, Welshmen, unitedly promote the prosperity of our native country.'

The work of extending the line still further west went ahead spiritedly, and by now Irish eyes, too, were watching its progress. When it reached Haverfordwest in 1854 the mayor of Waterford, Henry Denny, and two other local citizens attended the opening ceremony, where they expressed the hope that before long there would be 'a line of powerful steamers' plying between Milford and Waterford. Their wish was granted, for a steamboat service twice a week to Waterford started soon after the railway reached Neyland in 1856. 'Neyland is situated on the north-eastern shore of Milford Haven,' the *Illustrated London News* told its readers. 'It is the terminus of the South Wales Railway, which, joining the Great Western line at Gloucester, now forms a direct railway communication between the metropolis and our western shores.' The journey took nine hours, and the magazine said this development was expected to 'elevate Milford from being simply a harbour of refuge to the position of an extensive depot for maritime commerce.'

The line through South Wales, like the one along the North Wales coast, opened new doors. In 1857 tourist tickets were available at Paddington for 70s first class and 50s second class allowing people to stay three weeks in South Wales. In July of that year an excursion from Newport and Cardiff went to Cork for the regatta, the crossing from Milford being made by steamer. But pleasure parties went in the other direction too, and those joining an excursion from Swansea had a week in London with a trip to the Crystal Palace and Gardens thrown in. The charge was 29s 6d first class and 20s 'covered carriage'.

Classical scholars must have found a droll satisfaction in the names of the locomotives in use on the South Wales Railway at this time. In 1859 the *Hydra, Gorgon, Charon, Hecate* and *Medusa* — all belonging to the 2-2-2 Firefly class and built by Fenton, Murray and Jackson, Leeds, between 1840 and 1842 — were among the passenger engines, while the goods engines numbered the 0-6-0 *Bellepheron,* of the Premier or Ajax class, and *Caliban,* of the Pyracmon or Alligator class, in their midst. The *Hector, Alexander, Acheron* and *Phlegethon* pulled passenger trains, and so did the *Victor Emanuel* — a 2-4-0 locomotive of the Victoria class, built at Swindon in 1856. The *Trafalgar,* on the other hand, was a goods engine. Built in 1853, she was one of 26 engines of the Ariadne class and was to remain in service until 1871.

The locomotive superintendent of the GWR, Daniel Gooch, a hero in his own right who had been appointed to the job when only 21, drew up a list of locomotives in use on the South Wales line in September 1859. This showed that there were 22 passenger engines in steam, five spares and three under repair, and 19 goods engines in steam, three employed in banking and yard work, four spare and three under repair.

Brunel's broad gauge, however, which he had advocated so strongly for increased comfort and speed of travel, was fated to be only a passing phenomenon. The general preference for the 'narrow' gauge of 4 ft 8½ in. meant the gradual conversion of the GWR track after the Amalgamation Acts of 1863 brought the South Wales and other systems entirely within that company's control. In 1866, Gooch reported that they had received a petition signed by nearly every firm of standing in South Wales pressing for a change to the narrower gauge. As one of the original champions of the broad gauge he must have viewed it with sadness, but the writing had been on the wall for a long time.

Sir Daniel Gooch was first locomotive superintendent and then chairman of the GWR.

By 1870 plans for narrowing the South Wales gauge were well advanced, with all that entailed in the way of altering platforms, signals and sidings. The track itself — 188 miles of double and 48 miles of single — was converted in just over three weeks in 1872, and the *South Wales Daily News* showed a due sense of history:

'The Battle of the Gauges is drawing to a close, and the question which agitated railway engineers a quarter of a century ago is about to receive a definite settlement . . . In a few days the whole of the huge rolling stock will be 'off the line', and in course of being converted or broken up as old material. Brunel, the younger, if he were alive, would deeply regret a result which, deemed inevitable in his day, has at last been accomplished.'

A cartoon from 'Punch' published on June 4, 1892, entitled 'The Burial of the Broad-Gauge'. It was accompanied by some verses, one of which ran:

'No useless tears, though we loved him well!
Long years to his fire-box had bound us,
We fancied we glimpsed the great shade of Brunel,
In sad sympathy hovering round us.'

(By kind permission of 'Punch').

4 Rivals in the Valleys

THE PUBLIC RECORD OFFICE IN KEW, on the outskirts of London, holds official papers charting great events. It also contains letters which, humdrum enough at the time they were written, have achieved importance simply because someone with imagination thought them worth preserving when they might so easily have been thrown away.

Such a letter was written by John A. Godfrey, of Royal Terrace, Northampton, on September 6, 1845. He had just arrived home after two months on the Continent to find that a railway was contemplated through the Vale of Neath — a project which filled him with excitement. He wished to buy shares in it, but was afraid he might be too late. His only hope was the announcement that preference would be given to South Wales Railway shareholders. He wrote immediately to the secretary of the Provisional Committee of the Vale of Neath Railway Company stating: 'I venture though behind the fixed time to apply for 30 shares in that undertaking hoping that my abscence (sic) from England will not prevent my application being received as I hold 50 shares in the South Wales Railway.' The anxious Mr Godfrey added: PS. To assure you of my absence from England I enclose you my Passport which I will thank you some time to return to me.' Perhaps the unconscious humour of this postscript was responsible for the letter's preservation for so long before it reached the ultimate safety of the archivists.

So far as the purchase of Vale of Neath shares goes, Mr Godfrey was unduly worried. The public was in no rush to buy them, and when the company fell short of the required capital of £550,000 the South Wales Railway was able to step in with a subscription of £127,780, thus winning the right to appoint four of the eleven directors.

The Vale of Neath was a broad gauge line engineered by Brunel. It was a brave enterprise, designed to challenge the Taff Vale Railway monopoly of the mineral traffic of Merthyr. At first, however, the railway went only as far as Aberdare, the state of the money market and the problem of obtaining land postponing operations in the immediate vicinity of Merthyr. The directors were clearly on their guard against the exactions of land owners, for when the company secretary, Frederick G. Saunders — nephew of Charles Saunders, secretary of the Great Western — wrote to Thomas Stuck telling him of his appointment as land valuer for a portion of the line, he stated: 'The Directors desire that a fair and liberal compensation should be given in respect of any *real* damage which the formation of the Railway may entail on the Owners Lessees or Occupiers of the land required to be purchased — but they are determined to resist as far as they can the exorbitant claims which are now so frequently got up as Railway Compensation Cases to support which every imaginary grievance is invented.' Saunders added: 'The remuneration for your services will be 3 Guineas a day when employed on the business of the Company and that sum will cover every expense which you may incur between Neath and Merthyr Tydfil.'

The 19 miles to Aberdare from the junction with the South Wales Railway at Neath were opened for passenger trains on September 24, 1851 and for goods traffic three months later, the line being double to Hirwaun and single into Aberdare. The mountainous terrain gave Brunel plenty to think about, and the works included the 526-yard Pencaedrain Tunnel, some deep cuttings and several timber viaducts, one of which stretched 270 yards from the junction with the South Wales Railway in Neath. It was a steady uphill climb all the way from Neath to Hirwaun, with a gradient of 1:47 to 1:50 on the continuous bank of 5 ½ miles up from Glynneath. The original stations, as spelt at the time, were Aberdylais, Resolven, Glyn Neath, Hirwain, Merthyr Road and Aberdare.

The directors gave careful thought to the kind of locomotives needed on the line, and in June 1850 the GWR received a letter stating: 'The Line will need about *six* Engines of a description suitable for working a heavy Coal and passenger traffic over a gradient of *1 in 50*. Mr Brunel thought that an Engine something like the "last low-wheeled Engine made for the South Devon" would be the kind suited to the gradients. As regards carriages we should require principally *3rd* class but a few first and second class.* The Board are anxious to ascertain whether your Company would be disposed to supply this Company with the whole or any portion of the rolling stock they will require.' Charles Saunders replied saying that the GWR directors would be 'very happy to afford any facility which it is in their favour to give the construction of engines . . . at Swindon and generally to the building of rolling stock also.'

The company's own stock did not arrive in time for the opening of the line, however, so engines and carriages had to be borrowed from the GWR.

---

* In 1852, however, the company was providing covered first-class coaches as well as open excursion carriages 'specially adapted for viewing the justly celebrated scenery of the Valley and its tributaries.'

Meanwhile, the 'servants' of the Vale of Neath — as employees were generally known at the time — applied themselves to learning the rules, which was no small task. One of them stipulated that 'no servant of the company is permitted to reside or lodge at a public house, tavern or beer shop', while another read: 'The company's workmen in their working dress, persons afflicted with insanity or prisoners in charge of the police must not be put in with other passengers, but must be placed in a compartment by themselves.'

The days of corridor trains with toilets were in the distant future, but there was a clear instruction that on arrival at a station 'should any passenger require to alight for the purposes of nature, the guard must immediately permit him to do so, always urging upon him the necessity of resuming his place quickly, to prevent delay.' The danger of a sleepy or stupid passenger missing his station was also minimised. 'On arrival at each station,' employees were told, 'the first class passenger guard must go to every first class carriage window, and the second class passenger guard to every second class carriage window, and call out loudly and clearly the name of the station.'

The high moral tone of some of these rules was nothing unusual. The Taff Vale Railway rule book had the flavour of a religious tract. 'It is urgently requested that every person, whether on or off duty, shall conduct himself in

The Vale of Neath directors chose the broad gauge, which quickly went out of favour — and this is a fine example of the kind of broad gauge engine once a familiar sight on Britain's railways. (Pronto Photo History).

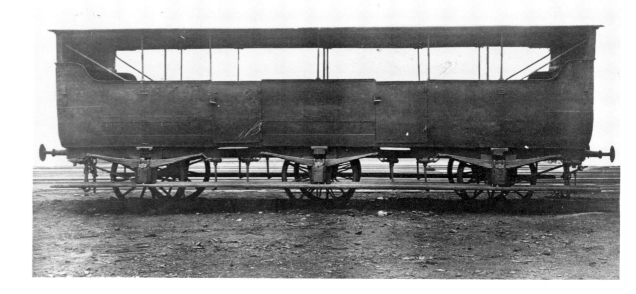

This Vale of Neath iron-bodied coach shows that creature comforts were at a premium in the early days of railway travel.
(Pronto Photo History).

a steady, sober, honest and creditable manner, and that on Sundays and other Holydays, when he is not required on duty, that he will attend a place of worship, as it will be the means of promotion when vacancies occur,' reads rule 26. Rule 40 went even further. 'Not any instance of intoxication, singing, whistling, or levity, while on duty, will be overlooked; and besides being dismissed, the offender will be liable to punishment.' This was immediately followed by: 'Any person drinking, sleeping, using improper language, or cursing and swearing, while on duty, or receiving money in the shape of a fee, or reward, will be liable to dismissal.' And cleanliness was clearly next to godliness. 'Every person is to come on duty daily, clean in his person and his clothes, shaved, and his shoes blacked.'

There was regulation clothing. Passenger guards on the Vale of Neath were issued with a greatcoat, frock coat, two waistcoats, two pairs of trousers, two pairs of boots and a cap annually. The company police had a dress coat, two pairs of trousers, two pairs of boots, a stock and a hat annually, but their great coat and cape had to last them two years. The porters' capes, too, were renewed every other year — and those who failed to take proper care of their uniform had to answer for it. 'No man on leaving the service is to be paid any money due to him, until he shall have delivered up his clothes in as clean and perfect a condition as the period he has worn them will allow,' ruled the company severely.

The signalling instructions in these early rule books read curiously to the modern eye. The Taff Vale used Brunel's disc-and-crossbar signals, which for many years were standard on the GWR and survived almost until the end of the century in some places. They consisted of a tall mast with a disc at the top and a crossbar below and, with the aid of white, green and red lights by night, gave three indications, categorised with delightful simplicity of language as **All right, Caution** and **Danger.** Hand signals were also employed, the Vale of Neath rule book stating: 'The violent waving of any object by day, or of any light by night, denotes danger.'

It was over two years after the opening ceremony that the Vale of Neath Railway at last reached Merthyr, the 2,495 yard Merthyr Tunnel having proved a major obstacle. Two contractors failed and the company carried on the work with direct labour until W. Ritson, who had made the Pencaedrain Tunnel, completed the project. Coal brought down the line was shipped from Briton Ferry and Swansea, and the special problems this posed Brunel were described by his son Isambard in his biography of his father:

'The coal of South Wales is of a friable nature, and, in order to avoid the breakage consequent on the ordinary mode of shipping coal, by tipping it down a shoot, Mr Brunel introduced on a large scale the use of trucks carrying four iron boxes, each box about 4feet 8 inches cube, and containing two and a half tons of coal. At the docks machinery is provided by which each box is lowered down into the hold of the ship, and the under side being allowed to open, the coal is deposited at once on the bottom of the vessel.'

Powerful tank engines were used on the line, but the company's close relationship with the GWR was not to the liking of all the shareholders. At the half-yearly meeting in August 1863, one of them grumbled that since the amalgamation of the South Wales with the Great Western they were much worse off. They were treated in a very cavalier way, and were sent 'the old engines and the old carriages of the Great Western stock.' By this time, however, the Vale of Neath was in its final phase as an independent line, for it became part of the GWR system in 1865.

The fourteen years which had elapsed since the first trains ran up through Resolven and Glynneath had seen other railways reaching into the industrial valleys of South Wales. One of the most striking achievements was the building of the Crumlin Viaduct, a graceful structure so light and airy in appearance that a writer in the *Railway Times* remarked that one almost expected a gentle breeze to send it toppling into the valley. Its opening on Whit Monday 1857 brought a huge holiday crowd to the scene, the vast majority of the visitors being 'undoubtedly mechanics and labouring men accompanied by their wives and daughters', according to the *Monmouthshire Merlin.* Booths selling beer were set up in the fields, the viaduct was draped with flags and a floral archway bore the words 'Long life and prosperity to T. W. Kennard' — this being the contractor. The side shows included a rifle gallery, and two ballad singers cashed in by singing a song specially written for the occasion and selling the words for a penny. The chorus went:

Thousands have come from far and near
So full of youth and bloom,
To open the Great Crumlin Bridge
On the Glorious First of June.

It may not have been great poetry, but it captured the enthusiasm of the
moment. The viaduct, which spanned the Ebbw Valley, was 200ft high and

CAUTION, to Go Slowly, is shewn in the same way, by a **Green Light.**

ALL RIGHT, to Go On, is shewn in the same way, by a **White Light.**

26. **Hand Signals by Day.**

DANGER, to Stop,

is shewn by holding **both**

Arms above the head,

thus—

Hand signals were extensively employed in the early days of railways, as these extracts from a Vale of Neath Railway rule book of the 1850s show. (Cardiff Central Library).

Another example of hand signals from the Vale of Neath Railway rule book. (Cardiff Central Library).

CAUTION, to Go Slowly, is shewn by holding the **Right Arm** above the head, thus—

ALL RIGHT, to Go On, is shewn by holding the right arm straight out and pointing **across** the Rails, thus—

27. Hand Signals by Night

Are made by Hand Lamps with different colored Lights, thus—

1,588ft long, and was said at the time to be the cheapest railway viaduct for its size ever erected. It was also the highest viaduct in Britain and the third highest in the world. 'The piers consist of cast-iron columns clustered and braced together, with a superstructure of the type known as "Warren's Patent" triangular trussed girder', reported the *Railway Times*. The company responsible for this superb work, which was demolished in 1966 in spite of pleas for its preservation, was the Newport Abergavenny and Here-

*The Crumlin Viaduct was
opened in 1857 before a huge
holiday crowd.*
(Pronto Photo History).

ford Railway, which was opened in 1854 between Hereford and a junction with the Monmouthshire Railway near Pontypool. The viaduct was part of a westerly extension of the line from Pontypool Road to a junction with the Taff Vale at Quakers Yard, and the necessity for such an elaborate piece of engineering illustrates the daunting problems facing these railway pioneers when they flung lines across the valleys instead of following their natural course from north to south. In 1864 the line was extended to join the Vale of Neath at Middle Duffryn, near Aberdare, where Thomas Powell's collieries were producing the fine steam coal for which there was an insatiable demand the world over. The provision of mixed gauge on the Vale of Neath meant that the Newport Abergavenny and Hereford Railway, a 4ft 8½ in. line, was able to run trains all the way from Pontypool to Neath.

The Quakers Yard junction gave the TVR the advantage of access to the Midlands, but it also brought a minor problem which the Taff Vale superintendent George Fisher put before his directors in January 1858. 'Day' (return) tickets were available on the Newport Abergavenny and Hereford but not on the Taff Vale, which meant 'some little inconvenience being felt by passengers.' Someone travelling from Hereford to Merthyr and back, for example, had to book a return to Quakers Yard with the NA and HR, and single tickets between Quakers Yard and Merthyr with the TVR. 'I may remind the Board', wrote Fisher, 'that day tickets at reduced fares have not hitherto been adopted on this line, the single fares having always been considered sufficiently low.' Every Whit Monday, however, the company was in the habit of going one better than a day ticket by issuing 'to and fro' tickets, which amounted to a return journey for the price of a single.

By this time the TVR had increased considerably in complexity and prosperity. In 1847 it had taken over the Aberdare Railway, originally a separate company under the chairmanship of Sir John Guest, and the extensions into the Rhondda in the next decade meant that when the coal prospectors moved in there in a big way in the 1860s the TVR became wealthy beyond the dreams of its promoters.

Meanwhile another important name had appeared on the Welsh railway map — that of the Rhymney Railway. It was incorporated in 1854, the preamble to the Act stating that 'a railway from Rhymney, in the County of Glamorgan, to a point of junction with the Newport Abergavenny and Hereford Railway would be of great public advantage by opening an additional and expeditious means of communication between the town of Rhymney and the rich mineral districts of the Rhymney Valley on the one hand, and the ports on the north side of the Bristol Channel and other places on the other hand.' The 'point of junction' with the NA and HR was Hengoed.

In the following year an Act was obtained extending the railway nine miles further south to join the TVR at Walnut Tree Bridge, Taffs Well, and obtaining running powers from there into Cardiff over the Taff Vale line. A branch line a mile and a quarter long took the Rhymney into the East Dock, then being built by the Marquis of Bute's trustees. Thus the new company gained entry to the port of Cardiff, which had rapidly grown in importance since the historic opening of its first dock, the Bute West, in 1839. In their report to shareholders in February 1858, the directors buoyantly observed: 'Your railway, when completed, will afford to the public the shortest route without break of gauge from the port of Cardiff to Hereford, Chester, Liverpool, Leeds and other important towns and districts in England, and should command a considerable local and through traffic in passengers, goods and minerals.'

The local press took up the same theme, remarking that 'drapers, clothiers and others doing business in the great hives of industry in Lancashire, Yorkshire and Warwickshire may be conveyed on an unbroken narrow gauge* in an almost incredibly short space of time.' The goods they ordered would be 'delivered at Cardiff without any change of carriage from the time they leave Manchester until they arrive here.' The *Monmouthshire Merlin* was more interested in the future of Caerphilly, which, being linked with the Walnut Tree junction by a branch just over a mile long, stood to benefit considerably. 'The opening of the Rhymney line will be hailed with joy by hundreds who now find it difficult and expensive to visit the venerable ruins of Caerphilly Castle,' the paper observed. 'This sequestered spot is one of the most delightful places for pic-nic parties, who may enjoy a rustic dance upon the castle green remote from the noise and bustle of commerce.' On a less idyllic note, the writer continued: 'Besides this, large collieries will be brought into operation, as all the neighbourhood teems with mineral wealth and with excellent house and steam coals.'

It was the potential coal traffic that inspired the Bute trustees to take the initiative in promoting the Rhymney Railway. They owned extensive mineral rights in the valley and saw the East Dock as an outlet for Rhymney coal and iron. One of the Bute trustees, John Boyle, became the company's first chairman, and two of the original directors of the railway were Henry Austin Bruce, later Lord Aberdare, and John Nixon, a pioneer of the coal export trade in South Wales.

The line took longer to complete than expected, one explanation being that labourers had abandoned the work to help with the harvest. The difficulties encountered at the Nantgarw cutting provided a more legitimate reason for delay. The works involved a million cubic yards of earth, and bad slips occurred in the wet weather. The other works of importance were a ten-arch viaduct at Pontlottyn and a seven-arch viaduct at Pont Aberbar-

---

* The gauge was, in fact, the standard gauge of 4ft 8 ½ in., which was commonly called 'narrow' before the 7ft broad gauge went out of existence.

The Rhymney No. 5, about 1890.
(J. P. Smith).

goed, the latter carrying the railway over the Rhymney river and a road at a height of 66 feet.

The line was opened, first for goods traffic only and then for passengers as well, in 1858. Originally it was single throughout, the passenger station in Cardiff being in Adam Street, on the Dock branch south of Crockherbtown (Queen Street) junction. There were three passenger trains each way on weekdays at first and two on Sundays, the journey of 24½ miles taking about an hour and a half. The original intermediate stations were Walnut Tree, Caerphilly, Ystrad Mynach, Hengoed, Pengam, Bargoed and Tir Phil.

The company was slow to prosper, for the coal trade was going through one of its periodic depressions, and it was five years before the shareholders received a dividend. In time, however, it became one of the wealthiest railways for its size in the country, declaring double-figure dividends on nine occasions between 1880 and 1899. A hard-headed Scot, Cornelius Lundie, can take much of the credit for this. For over 40 years he was company secretary and accountant, and if a penny was wasted he wanted to know why. He claimed to have 'examined every inch of the railway', and was equally proud of the fact that in spite of its severe gradients, there were only two fatal accidents during his term of management. Lundie, who gave rewards to drivers who brought down the largest number of wagons with the smallest consumption of fuel, had a softer side to his nature which was not always apparent to those who worked under him: at Robbie Burns banquets he considered himself as jovial as the youngest guest, and one of his proudest boasts was that he had shaken hands with Sir Walter Scott.

The Rhymney Railway made itself independent of the Taff Vale with its direct line to Cardiff through Caerphilly Mountain. The tunnel, one mile in length, took five years to complete and claimed several lives. On one occasion a skip plunged 117 yards down a shaft, killing its seven occupants, and a much worse tragedy was only narrowly avoided when a torrent burst through a limestone fissure. The men were in danger of being buried in a ghastly mixture of mud and running sand, but they managed to escape. The pumps were overwhelmed and water rose so high in the shafts in the northern half of the tunnel that the work there was suspended for three months. The constant flow of water in the mountain was eventually harnessed by means of pipes laid along the railway from the centre of the tunnel, the 60 million gallons yearly thus obtained being enough for the whole of the company's goods engines in Cardiff.

The first trains ran through the tunnel in April 1871, and in September of the same year the Rhymney to Nantybwch extension was opened to link up with the Merthyr, Tredegar and Abergavenny railway of the London and North Western Company. Both the Rhymney and the LNWR benefited considerably from this development, for it gave the former access to the ironworks and collieries in the north of the coalfield and the latter direct entry to Cardiff by means of running powers over the Rhymney system. The LNWR built a goods depot at the docks and carried a large traffic to and from the Midlands and the North of England, which meant a significant addition to Cardiff's trade. The Rhymney tapped further wealth by opening a short branch from Ystrad Mynach to Penallta, thus entering the Aberdare Valley by an exchange of running powers with the GWR, and in 1876 the Taff Bargoed Railway was opened. This was jointly owned by the GWR and Rhymney and gave access to the Dowlais ironworks and collieries. Six years later, the shrewd commercial brain of Cornelius Lundie engineered yet another money-making venture: a joint line with the GWR from Quakers Yard to reach the Cyfarthfa ironworks and collieries in Merthyr and the Merthyr Vale Colliery owned by Nixon's.

The complexity of the arrangements bewildered the layman and even made railwaymen scratch their heads. Telling the story of the Rhymney Railway at the time of the groupings which followed the First World War, the *Great Western Railway Magazine* observed that within seven miles of the Rhymney Railway terminus at Roath Basin Junction there were no fewer than eleven junctions with seven different companies:

'Several generations of traffic men and accountants have struggled with the resultant problems at great cost of temper and time, not to say money . . . It has always been a source of wonder . . . why the small lines of South Wales were so continuously fighting each other in Parliament — every session a

Opposite, top right:
*Rhymney Railway H and I
class engine, 1872.*
(National Museum of Wales).

batch of bills and petitions from each; but a survey of the Rhymney Railway with its junctions, running powers, joint railways, working agreements, and agreements that would not work, remove any cause for wonder except, perhaps, as to where the dividend came from.'

The history of the Rhymney, in fact, was one of continual struggle against the powerful interests that hemmed it in on either side. It possessed no docks of its own and, unlike most of the South Wales lines, did not have the advantage of following the course of a valley to the sea, thus securing a falling gradient for loaded trucks. Coal trains for Cardiff had to climb severe gradients, and on downhill stretches the gradients were so steep that the use of wagon brakes cancelled out any advantage. In fact, of the total length of 77 miles 12 chains worked by Rhymney engines, only a short distance was on a gradient less than 1 in 100. The Dowlais line rose continuously for seven miles at 1 in 40, then fell towards Dowlais at 1in 60, and the company boasted two of the highest stations in Britain — Cwmbargoed, 1,250ft above sea level, and Rhymney Bridge, 1,100ft. It is no surprise, therefore, that most of the mineral trains were worked with two or three engines, and that those on the Dowlais line needed four. The load for an engine climbing the bank to Cwmbargoed was limited to eight to ten wagons, yet in 1913 the Rhymney company carried 400,000 tons of iron ore and iron over this section.

It was regarded as a triumph on the part of the Rhymney to retain its independence so long, when so many of the smaller companies were forced to seek shelter against the fierce winds of competition by absorption and amalgamation with larger lines. Strict economy was the keyword. The stations were plainness personified, and it was said that the head offices were 'a triumph of utilitarian science rather than architectural achievement.'

At the time of absorption by the GWR in 1922 the company had 123 locomotives. Sixty-one of these were of the saddle-tank type and the remainder side-tanks, which weighed between 60 and 70 tons and were 30 per cent more powerful than the saddle-tanks. The coaches in regular use on the workmen's services included 40 to 50 owned and maintained by the colliery companies.

Among the company records which have survived the years are the names and wages of drivers and firemen. They show that employees sometimes had their pay drastically reduced. John Thomas, for example, was earning 7s 6d a day in 1893 before having his rate cut to 5s a day when he was downgraded to shed pilot driver. John Coles had a chequered career, being reduced to fireman in June 1886 because of a misdemeanour and having his pay cut from 4s 6d to 4s a day. In November he was reinstated for pilot work at 5s a day and ten years later he was earning 7s 6d a day. William Williams, on the other hand, may have been a model employee. His pay rose from 5s to 7s 6d daily between 1874 and 1882 and in 1902 he reached the giddy heights of inspector at 9s a day.

Opposite, bottom right:
*Brecon and Merthyr Railway
locomotive Hercules, built by
Sharp, Stewart and Co., in
1871. It was withdrawn in
1899 and sold to the Bute
Works Supply Co., in Cardiff
in 1900.*
(National Museum of Wales).

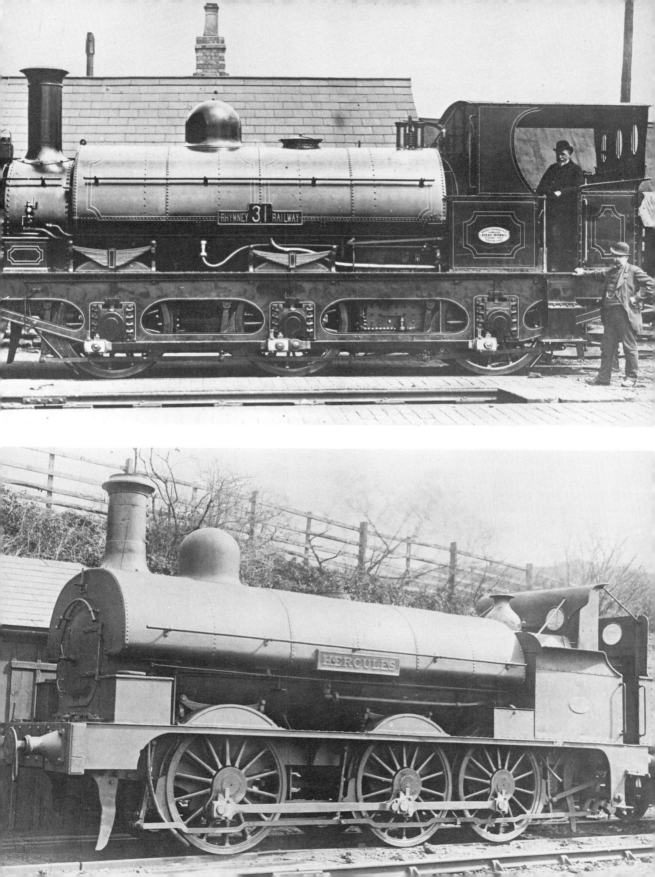

A sign of the rail amalgamations following the First World War — a late Rhymney P Class now belongs to the GWR.
(Pronto Photo History).

(Pronto Photo History).

CARDIFF.

TO BE SOLD BY

AUCTION,

(Under a Distress for Poor Rate), at the

RHYMNEY RAILWAY CO'S. FITTING SHEDS

ON THE EAST SIDE OF THE

EAST BUTE DOCK, CARDIFF,

AT ELEVEN FOR TWELVE O'CLOCK,

On Tuesday, the 1st day of January, 1867,

A LOCOMOTIVE PASSENGER

ENGINE

of the best construction, built in the
year 1858, No. 7.

D. DUNCAN, "CARDIFF TIMES" STEAM PRINTING OFFICES.

Thomas Brean had no such luck. In 1892 his pay rise from 3s 9d to 4s daily was withheld for two months 'owing to neglect of duty and losing time,' while James Norman also had to wait for his rise 'owing to having lost his train in the morning on several occasions.' The fact that the rate for the job remained fairly constant over decades shows how steady the value of money remained in those pre-inflationary times. Even in 1919, engine drivers on the Rhymney were receiving only 7s a day.

Another line of great character was the Brecon and Merthyr, which boasted the highest railway tunnel in Britain — near Torpantau, some 1,313ft above sea level. The company had the personal touch, a working time-table of 1902 stating: 'Guard William Thomas must see that hand-brake of van is properly screwed down before the Engine is cut off.'

The railway belied its name, because although it was incorporated in 1859 as the Brecon and Merthyr Tydfil Junction Railway, its main line reached Newport through the conversion of the old Rumney tramroad and the acquisition of running powers over sections of the Rhymney and GWR lines. Travellers from Newport to Brecon saw an amazing variety of scenery, their 47-mile journey taking them from the harsh industrialism of the coalfield to the grandeur of the Beacons. Trains to Merthyr passed over two great stone viaducts at Pontsarn and Cefn, and the railway was graced with such names as Twynshon Evan Curve and Rising Sun Deviation.

It was a line of characters as well as character. Clements, a B & M driver, would do his best to outpace Will Thomas, of the Rhymney, as they drove their trains on opposing sides of the valley between Bargoed and Bedwas. A

The Manchester and Milford locomotive Cader Idris, taken about 1898.
(National Library of Wales).

The B & M's great stone viaduct at Cefn Coed. (Pronto Photo History).

guard was known to paint lace curtains on the windows of his van, and there was even a song about the B & M:

> Six and five times up to Dowlais,
> Six and five times back same way;
> Whenever I wass finish,
> I wass get no extra pay!

A cry from the heart, if ever there was one. After a goods train went out of control and hurtled down Seven Mile Bank to Talybont in a spectacular 'wild run' in 1878, it was found that the guard had worked from 5 a.m. to 8 p.m. one day and 4 a.m. to 12.10 p.m. the next. The train consisted of 36 wagons, 22 of them carrying coal, bound for Birkenhead, drawn by the tank engines *Hercules* and *Atlas,* with another tank engine, *Severn,* coupled behind the brake van. Only the fireman of the *Hercules* and the driver of the *Severn* survived. Amazingly, the Board of Trade inquiry was told that wild runs were frequent at this spot.

Seven Mile Bank, which rose from 385ft at Talybont to 1,310ft at Torpantau, was the most fearsome climb on this mountainous northern section of the B & M where there were gradients of 1 in 38 to 1 in 40. Such long banks proved expensive to work, and in the 1860s Sharp, Stewart and Co. provided the company with specially-designed tank engines which were extremely powerful for their time. They were saddle-tank engines of the Stephenson long-boiler type, able to haul ten loaded wagons and two vans — total 100 tons — at the regulation speed of 8 m.p.h. up Seven Mile Bank.

When the B & M opened in 1863, the *Cardiff and Merthyr Guardian* hailed it as 'decidedly the most picturesque and delightful railway ride to be

obtained in South Wales.' But a coachman, seeing the first locomotives puffing laboriously up into the Beacons, boasted that he could drive his four-in-hand along the turnpike road from Talybont 'and deposit his passengers almost, if not quite, as soon as the steam-horse would take them.'

The B & M survived a financial crisis in 1866, when its rolling stock was liable to seizure, and showed great tenacity in its rivalries with other companies. At one time the Neath and Brecon Railway complained that it denied them the use of a loop line by keeping the points locked. So far as these railway pioneers were concerned, all was fair in love and war — and business was a battle to be fought to the last dividend.

5 The Sugar Loaf Line

IN THE PIONEERING DAYS OF STEAM, some routes were destined for railways as clearly as the heir to a throne for a crown: Chester to Holyhead, for example, or the industrial valleys where the exploitation of minerals obviously demanded the newest form of transportation. Sometimes, however, a railway had the appearance of an act of faith rather than a sound investment, forging unlikely links between places which had hitherto been remote from one another.

Such a line was the Central Wales Railway, which crossed some of the loneliest countryside in the Principality to connect the border town of Shrewsbury with the port of Swansea. The men who engineered its humble beginnings could not have known that, in time, it would provide a through route from Euston to Swansea for trains of the London and North Western Railway, a company which absorbed many rivals only to be itself swallowed up in the amalgamations that followed the First World War.

The unexpected success of the line in Edwardian times was due to the partiality of the English middle classes for the sea air of Pembrokeshire and the recuperative waters of Llandrindod Wells. There were through coaches to Carmarthen, Tenby and Pembroke Dock from Manchester and Crewe, and the rapid development of Llandrindod as a spa brought crowds of visitors by every train, a large proportion of them travelling first-class. There was so much luggage to be removed from the guard's van that the trains always stopped there for at least five minutes, even though the time officially allowed might be less, and the delay sometimes extended to a quarter of an hour or more, the difficulties of the single line adding to the problems. The station was a scene of opulence and elegance, with smartly-clad hotel porters in cloth of gold bowing to the whims of their social superiors. During the season at least three through coaches were run from Euston, and an 0-6-2 tank engine from Builth Road was employed in shunting the newly-arrived stock, two of the coaches being detached at Llandrindod to be put on the up trains next day.

It would have taken a visionary of exceptional powers to foresee such displays of luxury when the Knighton Railway, the first link in the chain that was eventually to unite Shrewsbury and Swansea, was born in 1858. It was one of a number of railway projects mooted in Mid Wales in the mid-century, some of which owed more to fancy than firm endeavour. The line ran only 12 miles from Knighton in Radnorshire across the border to Craven Arms in Shropshire, but it was always the intention of the promoters to extend the line west towards Llandovery. The significance of Craven Arms is that it stood on the Shrewsbury to Hereford Railway, thus holding out the promise of communication between south-west Wales and the English 'hives of industry' in the Midlands and North. Work on the line was delayed by the harsh winter of 1859/60 followed by a wet summer, the scarcity of labour adding to the difficulties. In October 1860, however, the first nine miles from Craven Arms to Bucknell opened, and by March 1861 the entire length from Craven Arms to Knighton was in operation.

The name of Central Wales Railway was at first applied only to the 19 miles of track between Knighton and Llandrindod, a scheme which received Parliamentary approval in 1859. The promoters included many of the local magnates who had initiated the Knighton Railway, and they had the satisfaction of knowing that they had beaten off a challenge from a rival company which seriously threatened their plans to take the railway on to Llandovery. This was the Mid-Wales Railway, which was refused consent to build a line from Builth to Llandovery running parallel with the one the Central Wales had in mind. The directors of the latter put this forward as 'strong evidence of the merits of their scheme, as affording the best line of communication from Manchester and the Midland districts, to the western coast of South Wales.'

The works between Knighton and Llandrindod began in 1860, and in the autumn of the following year it was reported that operations at the Knucklas viaduct had 'progressed materially'. The 13-arch viaduct, 190 yards long, was built of local stone in castellated style and regarded as 'a distinct architectural acquisition to the natural beauty of the country'. A three-mile ascent at 1 in 60 followed, leading to the 645-yard Llwyncoch tunnel. The line then reached a level stretch which, at 955ft, was the highest altitude between Llandovery and Shrewsbury, before descending a 1 in 100 incline to Dolau, just north of the Radnor Forest. The 440-yard Penybont tunnel was the principal work between Dolau and Llandrindod Wells.

The two miles of single track between Knighton and Knucklas were being worked by mineral trains in 1861, passenger traffic beginning the following year, but it was October 1865 before the entire length from Knighton to Llandrindod was opened. By then work on the next section, from Llandrindod to Llandovery, was well under way, and this remote line running through the hills of Mid Wales had won the attention of London journalists.

A stopping train from Swansea passes at Cynghordy.

The *Illustrated London News* assured its readers that 'the opening of the Central Wales Railway from Knighton to Llandrindod in October, with the approaching completion of the extension line from Llandrindod to Llandovery, bringing the Midland counties of England into more direct communication with the mineral districts of South Wales, and making the pleasant watering-places and the picturesque scenery of South Wales more accessible than they have hitherto been, is an event of general importance to the whole country.' The railway promised to obtain 'a large amount of traffic and to be very useful to the public, especially if Milford Haven should hereafter become a port of large American trade.'

The completion of 50 miles of track from Shrewsbury to Llandrindod was greeted with the rumbustious jollity so typical of the time. A special train drawn by two engines ran all the way from Shrewsbury, picking up Hereford passengers at Craven Arms. The band of the Radnorshire Rifle Volunteers travelled on the flag-bedecked train, playing stirring marches 'with the inspiration and harmony of true Welsh musicians'. One of the earliest rail magazines, *Herapath's Railway Journal,* noted that 'the country through which the line passed was a succession of mountains and valleys, affording some of the most romantic and beautiful scenery anywhere to be met with, but with a small and scattered population'. The writer, anxious to make the most of his Welsh safari, added: 'The course of the line was very winding and the curves very sharp, particularly immediately past the viaduct, where the trains described almost a semi-circle.'

The railway from Craven Arms to Llandrindod was worked by the London and North Western company, which had obtained powers in 1863 to provide locomotives and rolling stock for the combined Knighton and Central Wales lines, and its 2-2-2 tender engines built at Crewe were to become familiar sights in the Welsh hills in the years ahead. What attracted the company, however, was not the scenic beauty but the rich pickings which would come its way when the line at last connected with the industrial areas of Carmarthenshire and Glamorgan. The final link in the chain was the Central Wales Extension Railway from Llandrindod to Llandovery — for Llandovery afforded that vital access to Swansea and Llanelli.

The importance of this connection explains the celebrations that took place in Llandovery in November 1860, when the local friendly societies marched four abreast and Mr Batty's Menagerie and Circus Band brought up the rear of a procession that included the mayor and corporation. The occasion was simply the turning of the first sod of the Central Wales Extension Railway, but the excitement was such that it might have been the completion of the line. A colour party held the Union Jack, navvies carried picks and sledgehammers, and the shareholders displayed a banner saying 'Nothing Venture Nothing Win'. Another banner, summarising the faith in progress which was one of the tenets of the time, declared: 'Knowledge is Power'. Mrs Crawshay Bailey duly cut the first sod and even tipped the loaded wheelbarrow 'in capital style' after it had been run up a ramp, her presence being explained by the fact that her husband was chairman of the Vale of Towy Railway — the little line of such major concern to the LNWR.

Strictly speaking, the Vale of Towy ran only the eleven miles from Llandovery to Llandeilo, but it connected with and was worked by the Llanelly Railway, which itself had entry to Swansea via Pontardulais. So when the line to Llandovery was opened in 1868 there was more festivity, with parades and bonfires, and no less a personage than Richard Moon, chairman of the LNWR, as the principal guest. The traders and industrialists of Swansea with business in the North now had a direct route to Manchester and Liverpool via Shrewsbury, an early time-table reading: Swansea (Victoria) dep. 6.30 a.m.; Shrewsbury arr. 11.23; Manchester (London Road) arr. 2 p.m.; Liverpool (Lime Street) arr. 2.30 p.m. The 'Sugar Loaf Line', as the Central Wales affectionately came to be known, was complete.

The Sugar Loaf derived its name from the conical hill through which it passed near Llanwrtyd Wells. A tunnel 1,000 yards long was required, and a few miles away the line was carried on the 280-yard Cynghordy viaduct, another fine example of Victorian engineering consisting of 18 arches of 36ft span and costing £15,610. The challenge posed by the Sugar Loaf tunnel was one of the reasons the line took more than six years to complete instead of the anticipated five. There was an immense amount of water in the centre and an area of unstable rock extending a quarter of a mile. The tunnel, about

Dawn train crossing Cynghordy Viaduct in 1964 behind Standard class 5 No. 73026.

Morning train from Swansea climbing the Sugar Loaf Tunnel behind Stanier class 5 No. 45283.

800 ft above sea level, had the distinction of lying within both Breconshire and Carmarthenshire, the county boundary passing through the middle of it. Early travellers fearful of tunnels were rewarded by superb views down the valley the other side, the line falling 550 ft in seven miles to Llandovery. The author of an article in *The Railway Magazine* in 1912, C. N. Ryan, thought this 'one of the finest descents in the kingdom', describing how the train 'tears across the Cynghordy viaduct, flashes through the deserted station and on to Llandovery. Some years ago,' he continued, 'this incline was taken at a speed regularly touching 60 to 65 miles; but since the curve accidents at Salisbury and Shrewsbury it has been traversed at a much more cautious pace, never exceeding 40 miles per hour.'

Ryan gave an interesting account of the line at a time when the spas of Llandrindod Wells and Llanwrtyd Wells were in their heyday. The journey from Shrewsbury to Swansea by the quickest train was taking four hours, with 17 stops, and from Swansea to Shrewsbury three and a half hours, with only ten stops. Every train stopped at Knighton for a ticket inspection, which Ryan thought a pity, for 'not only does it take off momentum from the train for tackling the ascent, but spoils the run of the goods trains between

The Central Wales Line near the Sugar Loaf Summit. (British Railways).

Craven Arms and Llandrindod Wells. A few years ago the London and North Western Railway ran the old 1.30 p.m. from Euston through from Shrewsbury to Llandrindod with only one stop, at Craven Arms; but Knighton, with surprising vigour for a small place, objected so strongly that it had to be stopped.'

Llandrindod was 'the most valuable station to the London and North Western Railway on the line', and Builth Road, where the track crossed the Cambrian's Brecon-Llanidloes branch, an important junction with 'the dignity of an engine shed for about (*sic*) two little engines, which are used for helping heavy trains up the long incline to Llandrindod Wells'. Llanwrtyd was the busiest station on the line, next to Llandrindod, attracting many visitors from London and the North. The importance of Llandovery, however, must not be underestimated. 'It is here that the engines are stationed and all the goods trains are made up.'

The old Vale of Towy line to Llandeilo was, by that time, jointly owned by the LNWR and GWR, but between Llandeilo and Llanelli the line belonged solely to the GWR, the LNWR having only running powers. As a result none of the LNWR trains stopped at any of the five stations between Llandeilo and Pontardulais. 'At Pontardulais,' Ryan wrote, 'the Great Western goes off to join the main line at Llanelly, and the London and North Western, coming into its own again, proceeds to its station at Swansea, entering that town extremely picturesquely by the Mumbles.' There was a branch line from Llandeilo to Carmarthen along the Towy Valley through six small country stations. 'It is at present very unimportant; the trains are very slow, and except on market days, passengers few and far between. However, a few years ago it came in quite useful as an alternative route to Swansea, when during a tremendous storm the Great Western main line was severely damaged by the sea between Ferryside and Kidwelly. The authorities then ran the heavy Fishguard express up to Llandeilo and via Pontardulais to Swansea, where it got back on to Great Western metals.'

Since 1873 the greater part of the Central Wales line had been worked and owned by the LNWR, which found fast running extremely difficult because for more than half the way the track was single. According to Ryan, however, in the summer of 1911 the company had introduced a few large and powerful tank engines of the 'Precursor' type on the route, 'and it is no exaggeration to say that they "played" with the trains'. They were a considerable advance on the locomotives previously employed. 'For years the hauling had been done by old-fashioned tank engines of the type that vanished a few years ago from London and Watford trains. Compared with them, superheater engines "romp" along, and are always able to make up time, if only given a chance. Further accelerations,' he concluded, 'will do much to develop the traffic to this charming country.' Two years later the First World War broke out, to bring traffic of a different kind to Wales.

As we have seen, when the Central Wales was only a few miles of track in the Montgomeryshire hills its promoters had the grand vision of an iron road reaching from the industrial North and Midlands to the shores of Milford Haven. It was the kind of concept with immense popular appeal in that age of bravura, and it was preached with evangelistic fervour. As a result one of the most bizarre enterprises in the history of Welsh steam came into being — the Manchester and Milford Railway, which never went near either Manchester or Milford but ended up as the Pencader-Aberystwyth section of the Carmarthen-Aberystwyth line. The gulf between the dream and the reality was summed up, as it so often is, by a nickname — for the wags declared that the M & M really stood for 'Meek and Mild'.

The project did not fail for want of enthusiasm, for no fewer than 86

Standard class 5 No. 73090 emerging from Sugar Loaf Tunnel with the 11.45 a.m. from Shrewsbury in 1964.

directors were appointed. The year was 1845, and the country was seized by railway mania. With the ungovernable optimism that clouded the judgement of so many solid citizens at the time, they saw no insuperable obstacle in the way of laying a track across mountains and moors where even a post-chaise was a rare sight. The prize was tempting, for there were high hopes of turning Milford Haven into a port that would take a substantial part of Liverpool's trade. Its fine natural harbour had won the admiration of Lord Nelson; if the products of the 'dark Satanic mills' of Lancashire could be channelled through this new gateway to America, how could they fail? Alas for the dreamers of dreams ... the brightness of the vision inexorably dimmed until, in the end, they felt they were playing with shadows. For 15 years the company existed in name only, without a mile of track being laid. Then, in 1860, the company obtained an Act authorising a line from Pencader to Llanidloes via Tregaron, Strata Florida and Llangurig. It was a puny plan compared with the original, but it promised some reward in that other companies had by then forged links between Llanidloes and Crewe on the one hand and Pencader and Neyland on the other. Even this modest success, however, was beyond the capacity of the promoters. The first portion, Pencader to Lampeter, 12 ¾ miles in length, was opened for traffic on January 1, 1866, but at the northern end the heavy earthworks entailed by the mountainous country made for snail's-pace progress. At last, however, the line was carried three miles to Llangurig. Signals were erected, the contractors' locomotives puffed busily along the track, and preparations were made for the official opening. Suddenly, however, the work ceased for lack of funds, and eventually the rails were ignominiously torn up.

In the meantime, the line had been continued north from Lampeter to Aberystwyth, and on August 12, 1867, the first passenger train ran all the way up from Pencader. The contractor, David Davies of Llandinam, celebrated in style, for his shrewd brain told him that this was to be the sum total of the M & M's achievement — 42 miles of single track originally intended only as a branch line. He threw a dinner at the Belle Vue in Aberystwyth, declaring that 'Cardiganshire is at this moment hundreds of thousands of pounds more valuable as a county than it was when we first commenced the Manchester and Milford Railway.' He had a right to feel proud, for it was his money that had made even this limited achievement possible. When public funds dried up following the sensational collapse of the Overend and Gurney Bank in 1866, he put his own cash into the project. But he gambled only when the odds were in his favour, and refused even to contemplate bringing the line south-west from Llangurig.

Though its name remained forever an absurdity, the Manchester and Milford was a line full of character. It passed through a landscape which won the hearts of travellers by means of gentle persuasion rather than the thunderous rhetoric of Snowdonia. The strange beauty of Tregaron Bog, flecked with white cotton grass in late summer, had a haunting appeal, but nothing was more evocative than the name of Strata Florida station, which seemed to belong to another place and time. It was named after the Cistercian abbey three miles away, an eccentricity of choice which gave rise to some irritation. The inhabitants of Ystradmeurig, the village served by the station, felt strongly enough to organise a petition supported by the Earl of Lisburne of Crosswood (Trawscoed) Park and by people in several neighbouring parishes. This 'memorial' was submitted to the directors of the M & M on April 6, 1867, and showed that religious susceptibilities had been offended as well as local loyalties. It made the point that the station was within a quarter

David Davies at the age of 55. From an oil painting by Ford Madox Brown.

Inset:
David Davies, the one-time sawyer who became a symbol of Victorian thrift and enterprise in the construction of railways and docks and the sinking of coal mines.
(National Library of Wales).

mile of Ystradmeurig Grammar School, which had produced 'most useful members in the Church of England', whereas 'Strata Florida is a Latin name of the ruins of an old Abbey of Roman Catholic monks . . . three miles distant from your station'. It concluded: 'Even the people of the immediate neighbourhood could not make out why the station was named Strata Florida as the ruins are known to them only by its Welsh name of Monachlog Fawr.'

The directors stood firm. They were, perhaps, romantics at heart; or perhaps simply stubborn. Anyway, the name survived.

The best part of the M & M's business came from the holiday traffic between the industrial areas of South Wales and Aberystwyth. Writing in *The Railway Magazine* just before the company sold out to the GWR in 1906, T. R. Perkins reported: 'On the occasion of our visit, two heavy excursion trains, each consisting of eight or nine Great Western bogie coaches, left Aberystwyth in the evening on the return journey to Llanelly. Each train was packed with passengers, and was drawn by one of the ex-London and North-Western goods engines of the Manchester and Milford Railway.' Perkins remarked on the 'somewhat primitive white-washed buildings' of the majority of stations on the line, and the 'smooth and comfortable' travelling on the well-laid single track. He also dealt in detail with the rolling stock. The old No. 1 locomotive, *General Wood*, a six-coupled goods engine, had recently been sold. Two of the goods engines had been purchased from the LNWR, and were running without any alteration other than the removal of the number plates. No. 5, built in 1870, had six-coupled wheels, of 4ft 6in. diameter.

'With these exceptions,' wrote Perkins, 'all the engines are named. *Lady Elizabeth* is a six-wheeled, four-coupled tender engine, built in 1866, and has driving wheels 5ft 6in. diameter; No. 4, *Aberystwyth*, is a powerful six-coupled engine, built by Manning, Wardle and Co in 1868; while *Cader Idris* and *Plynlimon* are four-coupled double-end tank engines built in 1896 and 1891 respectively. They are all painted black, with orange lining, and their low-pitched boilers and curious bell-mouthed funnels give them a somewhat quaint appearance. The passenger coaches are painted a dark brown, with cream upper panels, and much resemble those of the Great Western Railway. Several of them run on bogies, the remainder having four wheels only; curiously enough, the upholstery in the four-wheelers is superior to that in the bogie coaches, the latter having no cushions for the back in the third-class compartments, though the seats are comfortably padded. In the four-wheelers both seats and backs are nicely upholstered.'

Negotiations between the M & M and GWR extended over several years. On November 9, 1903, J. C. Russell, general manager of the M & M, presented a 'suggested basis for a working agreement in perpetuity' to J. K. Rendell of the GWR. In an attempt to obtain the most favourable terms for his company, Russell detailed the savings the GWR could effect. By dispensing with the separate M & M posts of general manager, engineer, secretary, goods manager, superintendent and chief audit clerk, they would save a grand total of £1,150 a year in salaries and office rents. Moreover, the average annual running cost of an engine was £1,310 on the M & M, against only £1,072 on the GWR. 'This heavy cost is mainly due to the fact that the M & M company have no machinery or lathes of any kind and that all work not purely hand labour has to be put out and executed at works,' explained Russell. 'The difference in cost between the M and M Co and the GWR is £238 per engine, amounting on six engines to £1,428 per year. The wages of the staff employed in the locomotive carriage and wagon and stores department amounts to £1,240 per year. These shops could be closed and at least three-quarters of the wages saved, that is a saving of £930 per year. The above three sums amount to £3,508 annually and other savings could probably be effected.'

Rendell was not convinced. 'At all the interviews I have had with Mr Rendell,' complained Russell in a letter written later that month, 'he has spoken of present value as the determining guide: & the expenditure which he puts at £40,000 to bring the line into equal condition with the GWR: & the extra station working expenses as diminishing the value: and disregards the savings I pointed out.'

In 1906, however, the GWR secured the lease of the M & M and began working the line to Aberystwyth, where the town council showed its approval by congratulating the successful company. The local press was equally pleased, the *Cambrian News* stating that the 'greater facilities' of the GWR 'cannot but have a favourable effect on Aberystwyth'. The line would be worked from Swansea but the GWR would retain the M & M's offices in Aberystwyth, placing an agent and staff there. Some men, however, would be moved to larger districts. 'Eight of the old employees retire and as they are advanced in years and infirm it is understood that Mrs Berrow, who had great interest in the M & M, has kindly promised to provide for them.'

The other local paper, the *Welsh Gazette*, reported in its issue of July 5, 1906, that 'the driver and guard of the first passenger train on the M and M into Aberystwyth also brought in the last train on Saturday night. They are Mr Richard Jones and Mr Edward Edwards respectively, and both have been in the employ of the company during the whole period of its existence.' Richard Jones, who was an engine driver with the Cambrian Railways at the time the company could boast only a short length of track between Llanidloes and Newtown, was said to have distinct recollections of the fight between the promoters of the M & M and the Mid Wales Railway over the working of the line near Llanidloes. 'What one dug up during the day the other filled in at night, with the result that the poor M and M got thrown into Chancery,' reported the *Welsh Gazette* colourfully, if not entirely accurately.

Richard Jones — who at 63 was 'as young in spirit and as physically active' as ever — had joined the M & M in 1865, the year before it opened. 'He worked the contractor's ballast train, and assisted in the construction of the railway all the way from Lampeter to Aberystwyth . . . Although the M and M was remarkably free from any accident throughout its history, still Mr Jones had some thrilling experiences in his time. The greatest undoubtedly was when the boiler of his engine, the *Carmarthen*, burst at Maesycrugiau in the year 1890. He was working a mineral train at the time . . . The force of the explosion may be gathered from the fact that 12 cwt of the boiler was blown 400 yards into the River Teify (*sic*) where it is still to be seen when the river is low. The chimney was hurled into the fifth waggon from the engine. Mr Jones and his fireman had miraculous escapes, their injuries being slight. Mr Jones' cap was blown off his head and he never saw it again.'

The implication that the driver and firemen were in the immediate vicinity when the explosion occurred contradicts the stories told locally — for 90 years after the event, people still talk about it as if it had happened the day before yesterday. One version is that they were having a sly drink in the nearby pub when the boiler blew up. Another, more colourful, yarn is that news reached their ears — and they were both keen fishermen — when a friend was playing a big salmon in the river below. They ran to the scene, neglecting the engine with its banked boiler in their excitement. To this day, the spot where the boiler plunged into the river is known as Boiler Pool or Tank Pool.

Taking the railway across Tregaron Bog had caused the contractors severe problems. 'On one occasion,' the *Welsh Gazette* continued, 'the ground gave way under the ballast train and it was only with difficulty that the engine and trains were extricated. It took a fortnight to fill up the hole.'

Richard Jones regarded the vacuum brake as the greatest blessing ever bestowed on railwaymen. Before its introduction the descent of the Trawscoed gradient of 1 in 44 had been a risky task. 'Brakes would be put down hard at the top, but before the train had gone far these would be burnt out, and it was a case of trusting to Providence for the remainder of the descent. Many a time he came down the incline with no control over his train at all, and not able to pull up until Llanilar had been reached.'

With the advent of the GWR this stalwart had been placed in charge of a new engine from Swindon specially adapted for the heavy gradients between Aberystwyth and Pencader, but another of the veteran M & M drivers, Edward Benbow, had decided to call it a day. 'He had charge of the transportation of the first engine used on the line. It was brought from Caersws to Aberystwyth by the Cambrian Railway and then put on a huge trolley. The weight of the engine, named *Montgomery,* was 19 tons, and the trolley weighed 12 tons . . . It was an enormous undertaking to get this heavy load to Llanybyther but it was done with the assistance of some forty or fifty horses.

This engine was worked by Mr Benbow for the contractors and when the line was opened between Lampeter and Pencader he ran the first passenger train. Anyone who knew the M and M also knew the famous engine *Lady Elizabeth,* which commenced running in 1866 and worked regularly for 25 years, when she had another boiler put in and continued her useful career for another 15 years. It was only on Saturday last that she went out of steam for the last time, having been condemned by the Great Western company's officials.'

Benbow had driven 'The Lady', as he affectionately called her, throughout her active life, and their relationship had often been adventurous. There was the time when, returning to Aberystwyth one night, the train lurched fearfully near Llanybyther: part of the permanent way had been swept away by a flood, 'leaving the rails practically hanging on thin air'. Benbow sagely regarded the escape as providential. 'How the train got over this spot is a marvel.'

On another occasion the *Lady Elizabeth* left the rails near the Aberystwyth harbour siding and went over the embankment, where she lay on her side. Both driver and fireman stuck to their posts and fortune favoured the brave, for they emerged unharmed. The redoubtable Benbow also survived a winter journey when his engine was held up at night near Tregaron with the snow reaching nearly to the top of the boiler.

The Manchester and Milford engine Lady Elizabeth. Built in 1866 by Sharp, Stewart and Co.
(National Museum of Wales).

A Sunday School excursion from Aberystwyth to Lampeter almost ended in disaster when the train went out of control on the Trawscoed bank. It was before the time of the vacuum brake, so the only remedy was prayer as it rushed headlong down the Trawscoed bank with the children shrilling their delight. 'I never even saw Trawscoed station,' confessed Benbow, 'and we'd reached Llanilar before we could pull up.'

Such unseemly haste was untypical of a line which was the epitome of rustic tranquillity. It's true that before the First World War the GWR were running summer trains graced with the title of 'expresses' which stopped only at Lampeter, Tregaron and Strata Florida, but as a rule this was one of those routes where speed was secondary to sociability. Milk churns clanked, dogs scuffled, porters passed the time of day with passengers, and on every journey there was at least one station where, as in Edward Thomas's *Adlestrop:*

> The steam hissed. Someone cleared his throat.
> No one left and no one came
> On the bare platform . . .

There is the endearing, possibly apocryphal, tale of the man who sighed with relief as the train chuffed into Carmarthen and said feelingly, 'Well, thank God, that's the worst part of my journey over.'

'Where are you off to then?' asked the passenger sitting opposite.

'Hong Kong.'

When the line fell victim to the Beeching closures of the Sixties, something more than a rail service was lost. A part of rural Wales that had existed for a century, those familiar sights and sounds that give life flavour and a sense of continuity, also disappeared.

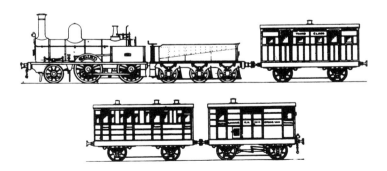

6 Cambrian Conquest

ONE OF THE MOST rewarding aspects of railway history is a study of the people involved, and the lines which eventually made up the Cambrian Railways could lay claim to some of the most colourful personalities of all. They had as contractors David Davies and Thomas Savin, men of violently contrasting temperaments who worked in harmony for years before quarrelling bitterly, and as a pioneer director George Hammond Whalley, whose religious bigotry was such that a newspaper published in the Roman Catholic interest was driven to describe him as 'a roistering, bawling, vulgar, brazen stump orator — self-conceited, arrogant, brainless.'

Of this trio, the man who achieved the greatest prominence was David Davies, whose name is linked inseparably with that of his native village of Llandinam. His was a classic case of Victorian thrift and energy being rewarded with boundless success in a diversity of endeavours. After beginning life as a humble sawyer he went on to build bridges and docks — and as a coal owner he was 'Davies the Ocean', head of the powerful Ocean combine in South Wales. The eldest of nine children, he had a prodigious appetite for work, sawing timber all day and helping out on the family farm at night. He married shrewdly though not for money, his wife, Margaret Jones, having the same chapel background as himself: she had the admirable if unlikely reputation of knowing the whole of the New Testament by heart, as well as the psalms and the Book of Isaiah.

Davies had achieved modest success as a contractor, building bridges and roads in Montgomeryshire, when at the age of 36 he made a crucial decision. Tenders were invited for making the first portion of the Llanidloes to Newtown Railway, the advertisement stating: 'Any contractor possessing a small quantity of materials may undertake the contract as the works are to be paid for in cash, by monthly instalments.' The plans and specifications were available for inspection at the company's offices in Llanidloes at 11 o'clock on the morning of October 2, 1855, and tenders had to be delivered to the directors only eight hours later. This presented no problems to David Davies, who had the knack of instant calculation: he knew at a glance how much timber a tree would yield, and at fairs he could state at sight the weight of a hog or bullock. His tender, the lowest of seven, was accepted, and his life thereafter was never the same.

The railway had first been projected in 1852 by a committee chaired by Whalley, who put himself at the head of the Montgomeryshire people anxious to keep local railways in local hands although he actually lived outside the county. He was the squire of Plas Madoc in Ruabon, Denbighshire, but was a magistrate for the three counties of Denbigh, Montgomery and Merioneth. With the GWR and LNWR extending their rivalry into Mid-Wales, where they put forward competing schemes, Whalley championed the town of Llanidloes in its determination to have a railway linking with any line made by either of the two giants. The irony is that Parliament rejected the GWR and LNWR proposals but approved the plan for a Llanidloes to Newtown Railway, 11¾ miles in length. The result was that this modest railway was built in the middle of nowhere, with no connection at either end to give it significance. 'People laughed because it had no head or tail,' a speaker was to admit at the opening ceremony. Yet, from the start, the grand design of a line from Manchester to Milford haunted the imagination of the promoters. Though isolated now, their little track might one day form a link in that 130-mile chain — and as we saw in the last chapter, the M & M scheme in 1860 did in fact envisage a line from Pencader connecting with their railway at Llanidloes.

David Davies made such a good impression on the directors of the Llanidloes & Newtown that, within a month, he had been given the contract for the second section of line, and before long the construction of the entire railway was entrusted to him. The nicknames of his two foremen have survived — 'The Preacher' and 'The Sentry' — but, unhappily, not the reasons they were called thus. In spite of the difficulties of making a railway in such isolated country (the materials were first brought by canal to Newtown and thence taken by horse-drawn transport to Llanidloes) the line reached Llandinam in August 1856, and one can imagine Davies's pride at being seen on his home territory in his new capacity of railway contractor. The shortage of cash, however, was becoming crucial, and the shareholders jumped at Davies's offer to lease the line. This signalled the arrival of the first engine, which he acquired for £400. It was hauled through the country lanes from Oswestry by fourteen horses, with another seven pulling the tender, and was an object of ardent curiosity as it stood for an entire Sunday in the High Street at Newtown; having arrived there on a Saturday evening, it could be taken no further until Monday morning because David Davies was a strict Sabbatarian.

By the end of 1857 the line had reached Penstrowed, three-quarters of the

Opposite:
David Davies in his latter years — one of the landed gentry. An expert shot, he is seen here with his favourite spaniel 'Midge'.
(Longmans, Green & Co.).

way to Newtown, but funds ran out and there was no work at all on the project in 1858. It was a period of enforced idleness for some, but not for David Davies. His fame had spread, and he went north to build the Vale of Clwyd line from Denbigh to Rhyl. He took with him his newly-acquired partner, Thomas Savin, an Oswestry draper of mercurial temperament. Savin's impatience was such that, when selling his wares at a Welsh mart where it was the farmers' custom to dispose of the livestock before looking around the stalls, he caused a sensation by rushing into the ring and buying a thousand sheep. Years later, when his flamboyance led him into deep waters, this tale was being told with relish as an example of his reckless impulsiveness.

David Davies's legendary strength was tested to the full on the Vale of Clwyd. He put in sixteen hours a day, to the astonishment of navvies who were not used to a master who subjected himself to such herculean labours. When the line opened on August 14, 1858, twelve of them were moved to present an address and a set of silver plate to Davies and Savin 'as a mark of esteem and appreciation'. It was not the last time the one-time sawyer was to receive such an accolade.

Early in 1859 Davies and Savin offered to complete the Llanidloes &

Thomas Savin — the draper turned contractor who was David Davies's partner in the pioneering days of the Cambrian Railways. His reckless speculations eventually led him into bankruptcy.
(Longmans, Green & Co.).

Newtown railway in return for all unissued shares and debentures, a canny move which meant a 25 per cent rise in their takings. Whalley demurred, but was overruled by the other directors, who had almost lost hope of seeing the line completed. The work resumed with the excavation of Scafell cutting, and was quickly completed. On August 31, 1859, the official opening took place.

It was a memorable day in the life of Llanidloes. Country folk gathered from miles around, houses were decked with flags and evergreens, and the Red Lion flaunted a banner saying, 'Welcome, Whalley, champion of our rights'. This was terseness personified compared with some of the other texts. 'G. H. Whalley, whose unceasing exertions are now crowned with success', declared a banner raised aloft in the public procession, which was not so much a slogan as a sermon. Another trumpeted bravely: 'Whither Bound? To Milford', while a third hailed 'The spirited contractors, Messrs Davies and Savin'.

Filled with civic dignitaries, the ceremonial train arrived in Newtown shortly after noon, where a leading shareholder, Mrs Anne Owen of Glansevern, near Berriew, was loudly applauded when she said that 'the iron road is destined to act beneficently in the humanising of nations, next only to Christianity itself'. At half-past three the company assembled again on the platform for the return journey, and when one or two gentlemen let the side down by taking their seats before all the ladies were accommodated 'they were very unceremoniously brought out again, amidst the ironical cheers of the outsiders'. At last the 48 trucks and carriages were crammed with an estimated 3,000 passengers and two engines, one of them the 0-4-2 saddle tank *Milford,* hauled the train back to Llanidloes. 'The appearance of this monster train was magnificent,' one account read. 'More than 2,000 of the passengers were in open trucks, and at certain points, where there was a curve in the line, and a good sight could be obtained, the train, as it wound its way through the valley, presented a scene not easily to be erased from the memory.'

The celebrations continued the following day, when a thousand guests were royally entertained by David Davies at Llandinam. They included the workmen who had built the line, and one of them was moved to sing several verses of matchless doggerel. Three of them went:

> Well now we've got a railway,
> The truth to you I'll tell,
> To be opened in August,
> The people like it well;
> We've heard a deal of rumour
> O'er all the country wide,
> We'll never get a railway
> The people can't provide.

Well now we have the carriages
For pleasure trips to ride;
The Milford it shall run us,
And Henry lad shall drive;
There's also Jack the stoker,
So handy and so free,
He lives now at Llandinam,
A buxom lad is he.

When these few days are over,
The navvies they will part,
And go back to their gangers
With blithe and cheerful heart;
And Jack he will be hooting,
And getting drunk full soon;
I wish there was a railway
To be opened every moon!

As the company stamped and roared their approval, Colonel Wynn stepped forward and bought a copy of this effusion for a shilling, which set an example several other gentlemen followed. To the chagrin of the performer, his supplies were limited.

The sight of a man of humble stock like David Davies entertaining on so lavish a scale appears to have disturbed the sensibilities of George Hammond Whalley, who had a high regard for his own social position and believed his descent from the first cousin of Oliver Cromwell was a matter of significance. His resentment found curious expression next day in a passionate outburst at the ceremony of cutting the first sod of the Mid Wales Railway at Rhayader, an enterprise in which the ubiquitous Davies and Savin had an important stake through their financial contribution. Whalley's temper was not improved by the fact that he had been thrown off the board of this company by votes and proxies mustered by Savin, and two days of junketing might well have made him liverish. The result was that after a ceremony conducted in a downpour, he made a scathing attack on Davies and Savin in the luncheon tent, saying he would never be the servant of 'contractors turned traders and monopolists'. There were angry exchanges and it was noted that the band played loudly whenever someone opposed Whalley. The ladies left hurriedly and as tempers rose, the waiters discreetly removed bottles and glasses from the tables. Ironically, the long delay in starting work on the line meant that Davies and Savin played no part in its construction.

Sir Watkin Williams-Wynn, a railway pioneer who had Wynnstay, a Llanidloes & Newtown engine, named after his estate.

Now that the Llanidloes to Newtown railway was a reality, the Newtown to Oswestry was not long delayed. Davies and Savin took over the contract from the bankrupt Davidson and Oughterson, paying off £45,000 of the

Newtown to Oswestry company's debts so that work on the line — delayed by difficulties in obtaining land — could begin again. A further delay was caused when the autocratic Mrs Owen of Glansevern refused to have the line anywhere near her home, although she had as big a stake in this company as in the Llanidloes to Newtown. As a result the line had to be diverted to the opposite bank of the river, which meant a two-mile bank up to Forden. In June 1861, however, a through-service from Oswestry to Llanidloes began.

In the meantime, Davies and Savin had parted company. The rift occurred when Savin became enamoured of a grandiose scheme to build a Welsh coast railway from Aberystwyth to Porthdynllaen, with luxury hotels in Aberystwyth, Borth and Aberdovey. The cost was astronomic, but Savin was convinced it was feasible because he imagined travellers could be inveigled into staying in the hotels by offering them rail tickets inclusive of board. To David Davies, the whole thing was lunacy. He saw his hard-won fortune being frittered away by a reckless adventure, and went to great trouble to extricate himself from any legal ties with Savin. Looking back on that unhappy period, he remembered the 'numerous useless journeys to London and elsewhere, when I could ill afford the time, in order to compel a dissolution and to secure what I could of my admitted share of the partnership property which was being rapidly absorbed in the vortex of speculative extensions and wild-goose schemes'.

Davies himself supported a simpler plan proposed by a Machynlleth solicitor, David Howell, for a line from Machynlleth to Aberystwyth linking with an extension to Towyn which the Corris Railway was considering. Most of the directors of the Newtown and Machynlleth Railway — the next link in the chain from the border country to the coast — backed David Davies, but the Oswestry to Newtown and Llanidloes to Newtown threw their weight behind Savin. The result was that Savin went west — in more senses than one — to make a line from Machynlleth to Aberystwyth, leaving Davies to build the Newtown to Machynlleth on his own. There was a dramatic scene at Machynlleth where Davies, standing on a wheelbarrow, told the assembled navvies that he and Savin were parting company. 'Now there's work for all of you, on either of the two jobs, and you can choose for yourselves. Those who prefer the Aberystwyth line with Mr Savin, stand to the right. Those for the Newtown line with me, go to the left.'

The navvies who plumped for David Davies had the memorable experience of gouging the Talerddig cutting out of solid rock. At the time it was the deepest cutting in the world, and its construction tested the nerve as well as the endurance of the workmen. Talerddig stood 693 ft above sea level on a flank of Pumlumon, the mountain mass which had clouded the visions of all railway promoters hoping to strike a path from Offa's Dyke to the sea. Davies preferred this 120 ft cutting to a tunnel for a very good reason — he needed large quantities of stone to bridge several deep ravines west of

Benjamin Piercy, who, with David Davies, engineered many of the early lines in Mid-Wales.

Talerddig, and the excavation of the cutting provided it. Before work could begin, however, a firm footing had to be obtained on the bog which enclosed it on three sides. Davies sent 200 men headed by one of his most reliable gangers, David Evans, who with the ingenuity and fortitude typical of the time managed to divert a stream flowing through the bog so that it joined the River Dovey instead of the Severn.

Talerddig haunted Davies. In London one night, he dreamt he saw water rushing into the cutting and woke with such a vivid sense of impending disaster that he hurried back to Wales to find that flood water was indeed pouring in. 'I often feared this would be the rock of my destruction,' he declared emotionally when it was finished, 'but with hard work and Heaven's blessing it has proved to be the rock of my salvation.' The remarkable hold he kept on the affections of his men in spite of the gigantic tasks he set them was seen in the efforts they made to complete the line on time. One director observed that they were 'treading upon each other's heels'. His secret was that he never asked anyone to do a job he could not do himself, and although he was forbidding when something displeased him he had an engaging capacity for fun. When there was time for such diversions he would challenge a workman to a wrestling match or weight-lifting contest, and in his early years as a railway contractor he would startle the men by crying 'Tally-ho, boys!' at the sight of a fox and join in the chase with them. His charisma was such that there were men who swore they would work for David Davies for sixpence a day less than they might receive elsewhere.

On May Day 1862 a contractor's train ran from Caersws to Machynlleth, but it was January 1863 before the line was opened for passengers. Two engines, the *Countess Vane* and *Talerddig,* which could haul 140-ton loads up 1 in 52 gradients at 15 miles an hour, drew a train of 22 carriages packed with 1,500 passengers to Newtown, with David Davies riding triumphantly on the footplate. The journey was enlivened by the panache of the young Marquess of Blandford, nephew of the company chairman, who stood by Davies playing 'See the Conquering Hero Comes' on his cornet. The engines had an even tougher task on the return journey, for there were no fewer than 36 carriages — 'a monstrous train,' said Davies at the feast in Machynlleth Town Hall, 'and it is something to be able to say that all who were in it felt perfectly safe.' At a private celebration for his workmen he slapped a bag of 500 sovereigns on the table. 'There now, my men,' he said, exulting in their astonishment, 'you have served me well. I am now going to make you a present of that bag of sovereigns.' He shared them out, some receiving five apiece and others as much as twenty-five.

Once again David Davies had proved a man of his word. He had completed the railway on time, and at the amazingly low cost of £9,000 a mile. The success gave him the self-confidence and financial basis to

Opposite:
The challenge of Talerddig summed up in a rare photograph. David Davies, in frock coat and silk hat, directs operations in the cutting.
(Longmans, Green & Co.).

Cambrian Railways passenger tender engine built by Sharp, Stewart and Co., in 1878. It was sold to the GWR with the amalgamations of 1922 and withdrawn in 1925. (National Museum of Wales).

consider new spheres of activity, and by 1870 his Ocean collieries in the Rhondda were in second place among producers of Welsh steam coal.

Meanwhile, his former partner had taken the first fatal steps towards bankruptcy. By August 1862 Savin's railway from Machynlleth to Aberystwyth had reached the sand dunes at Ynyslas, where he hopefully built a row of lodging houses only to see them start sinking as soon as they were finished — a commentary on the impracticality of his ways which a more philosophical man might have taken to heart. Autumn gales held up work to such an extent that the navvies became restive and extra police were drafted into the area. On 1 July 1863, however, the line was opened as far as Borth, then a tiny village entirely given over to seafaring. The arrival of the Aberystwyth & Welsh Coast Railway was viewed with suspicion by some of the natives, but the mood in Aberystwyth was one of jubilation. The towns-people had given the scheme their enthusiastic support, for they were acutely conscious of the fact that rival resorts along the North Wales coast had enjoyed rail facilities for over a decade. On the day the first train ran crowds made their way from Aberystwyth to Borth in all kinds of vehicles, and those unable to obtain seats formed a mile-long avenue to cheer the lucky ones on their way. Typically, the passengers expressed their delight by singing hymns.

The railway's arrival on the shores of Cardigan Bay was something of moment not only for Aberystwyth but for the people in the Welsh Marches now within easy reach of the sea for the first time in their lives. A Shrewsbury newspaper advertised 'six hours by the seaside for half a crown'

— the return excursion fare from Shrewsbury and Oswestry. One day all the tickets were exhausted but Burke, the Irish stationmaster at Carno, booked thirty or forty farm labourers with cattle tickets. When reprimanded by higher authority for 'making beasts of them', he defended himself by saying that many of them had made beasts of themselves that day without any help from him. These excursions, in fact, had a liberating effect. 'Boats are in great request and the ladies cling very lovingly to the boatmen who, in return, hug them very tightly as they embark or disembark their fair freight,' observed a newspaper correspondent. He even saw a bevy of nude beauties 'waddling like ducks into the water', and felt obliged to express whimsical disapproval. 'The porpoises were alarmed and betook themselves off. And so did we. Had the bathers been black instead of white we should have thought ourselves on the coast of Africa. Such an Adam and Eve-ish state of things we never saw before. Well, "honi soit qui mal y pense." '

The line from Borth to Aberystwyth was opened on June 23, 1864, when the first train into the town was accorded a civic welcome. The wine and the oratory flowed so freely at the ceremonial banquet at the Belle Vue Hotel that it was 11 p.m. before the company could be persuaded to take their seats in the return train, which meant that some dignitaries rolled into Oswestry at the very undignified hour of 3 o'clock the next morning. It had been a memorable day which had seen the opening not only of the line but of Savin's new hotel in Borth. The completion of the track between Oswestry and Ellesmere in the next few weeks meant that by the end of July, through running from Whitchurch had been established.

The amalgamation of the companies that made up the chain of railways

The Cambrian Railways locomotive Mountaineer, built for the Oswestry and Newtown Railway in 1863 by Sharp, Stewart and Co. (National Museum of Wales).

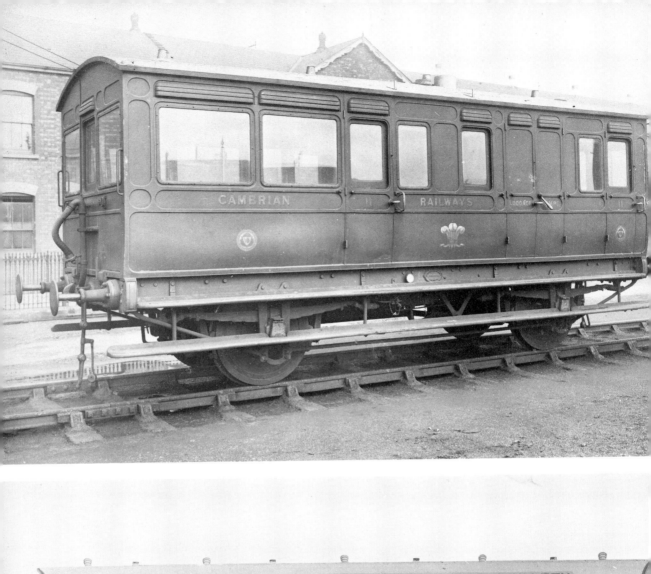

CAMBRIAN RAILWAYS

OBSERVATION CAR. PWLLHELI. BARMOUTH & MACHYNLLETH

4072   THIRD   G W R   THIRD   4072

Llanidloes and Newtown Railway engine, Wynnstay, 1859. It was taken over by the B and M Railway about 1866 and withdrawn in 1884. (National Museum of Wales).

from Shropshire to Cardigan Bay had long been in the air, and it took effect in that summer of 1864 with the incorporation of the Cambrian Railways Company. This consisted of the Oswestry & Newtown, the Llanidloes & Newtown, the Newtown & Machynlleth and the Oswestry, Ellesmere & Whitchurch Railway — 83¼ miles in all, the Aberystwyth & Cambrian Coast being excluded for a year for legalistic reasons. Savin's star was high — but eighteen months later, his financial affairs were in ruins. He had over-reached himself by his continual acceptance of shares instead of cash and his prodigious expenditure on fanciful schemes such as the creation of the Castle Hotel in Aberystwyth, the florid architectural style of which was to be masterfully summarised as 'early marzipan'. This colossal folly, with its mock-Gothic towers and pinnacles, had a strange destiny. Instead of being a luxurious retreat for the wealthy it became the 'College by the Sea' after the newly-fledged University of Wales bought it for the bargain sum of £10,000 — only a fraction of its cost — in 1872.

Savin's crash in February 1866 was a personal disaster which shocked Wales and threw the affairs of the Cambrian into confusion. Savin had, by then, achieved the considerable feat of carrying the railway along the sheer cliffs north of Llwyngwril, where the perils were such that he employed sailors to help carve the track bed because they had a head for heights. Further south, however, passengers were still being ferried across the Dovey estuary from Ynyslas to Aberdovey, the rail connection via Dovey Junction

Opposite, top:
Primitive by today's standards, but 19th century travellers stepped happily into coaches like this. (Pronto Photo History).

Opposite, bottom:
GWR directors made the most of the scenic beauties of the Cambrian Coast line. (Pronto Photo History).

*Cambrian Railways
locomotive No. 98.
(National Library of Wales).*

not being made until August 1867. The original plan had been for a huge bridge across the Dovey estuary from Ynyslas to Aberdovey, where it was hoped to establish a regular service of steam boats to Ireland. The shifting sands of Ynyslas, however, and the tempting presence of nearby taverns, defeated this bold conception: the men seeking a firm foundation with boring rods could work only at low tide, and by the time the waters receded they were in such a state that they scarcely knew if they were standing on solid earth or not.

The Cambrian's financial crisis worsened three months after Savin's bankruptcy with the failure of the discounting house of Overend & Gurney, but the company survived and eventually the railway was taken to Barmouth by means of an 800-yard viaduct constructed on timber piles driven into the sand.* Locally this was regarded as an engineering miracle: one august resident was so convinced of the impossibility of the scheme that he promised to eat the first engine that crossed the Mawddach Estuary. He happened to be among the passengers when the first train made the journey in 1867, and was taken to a table laid for one and politely asked if he wanted the engine roast or boiled. Sadly, he failed to appreciate the joke.

The railway was taken to Porthmadog and Pwllheli — the dream of reaching Porthdynllaen was never fulfilled — to complete a coastal line which became justly famed for its scenic grandeur. As the tradition of a summer holiday by the sea became established in the latter part of Victoria's reign the company's status and prosperity rapidly increased, and ticket offices were set up in Liverpool, Manchester, Sheffield, Birmingham and Cardiff. Cinema and lantern lectures also figured in the publicity drive.

---

* The bridge was rebuilt between 1899 and 1909, when the eight iron spans were replaced by four of steel, one being a swing bridge of 113ft providing two shipping lanes.

To cope with the traffic, the Cambrian expanded its locomotive stock from 58 to 85 between 1888 and 1898. The new engines were more powerful than the existing stock, much of which was rebuilt with bigger boilers. New carriages were also acquired and gas lighting was standard from 1894, but foot-warmers consisting of tins filled with hot water were commonly in use as late as 1912. The fact that lavatories were not introduced on ordinary coaches until the 1880s must be judged by the standards of the time rather than taken as indication of unconcern. In many ways the Cambrian was acknowledged to be ahead of the times in its provision of creature comforts, such as refreshment rooms on station platforms. Its employees, however, were expected to work the arduous hours which were the common lot of railway workers. They put in 152 hours a fortnight — yet some companies were even harder taskmasters, with a 90-hour week. The Cambrian found itself in deep water after dismissing a stationmaster, John Hood, who had insisted on defending a porter dismissed after a derailment at Ellesmere. The porter had been on duty 19 hours and Hood gave evidence before a Select Committee of the House of Commons looking into the excessive hours worked by railwaymen. This infuriated the directors, who gave him a month's salary in lieu of notice, thus incurring the wrath not only of the Amalgamated Society of Railway Servants but of the Commons itself which found that the Cambrian had been guilty of a breach of privilege by acting in a way calculated to deter other railway employees from giving evidence. The

Insert:
The down Cambrian Coast Express at Westbury.
(Pronto Photo Library).

Morning express entering Welshpool from Aberystwyth on the Cambrian Railways.

Above: *Montgomery Station. John Thomas collection.* (National Library of Wales).

Below: *Machynlleth Station, one of the historic John Thomas collection at the National Library of Wales. Thomas travelled through Wales in the last decades of the 19th century photographing Welsh life and personalities. His photographs, on glass negatives, were taken between 1870 and 1905.*

Above: *A Workman's Train on the Festiniog Railway, John Thomas collection.* (National Library of Wales).

Below: *Trawsfynydd Station. John Thomas collection.* (National Library of Wales).

directors were called to the Bar of the House and admonished by the Speaker to conclude one of the darker chapters in the company's history.

In the years immediately preceding the First World War the Cambrian ran a great many troop trains for Territorials attending summer camps in the Aberystwyth area. When war came the rumble of coal trains was continually heard on the company's Mid Wales line, no fewer than 250 of them heading north every night to take fuel to the Grand Fleet at Scapa Flow in 1918. Thousands of tons of war equipment and general stores were handled by the Cambrian, and the amount of timber carried from Welsh forests increased from 21,000 tons in 1914 to 172,000 tons in 1918.

The Cambrian was not the easiest line to work. It had steep gradients and mostly single track — a hazard which gave rise to the Abermule disaster of 1921, described in a later chapter. Punctual working was almost impossible, but on the eve of amalgamation with the GWR in 1922 the company could boast of eight trains in every ten arriving within five minutes of schedule. By that time the Cambrian, with 300 miles of track and operations extending from Pwllheli in the north to Merthyr in the south, had become the largest independent Welsh company.

By a happy chance the last chairman of the Cambrian was Lieut-colonel David Davies, MP — grandson of the sawyer turned contractor who laid the first lengths of track. History, at times, has an engaging alliance with sentiment.

Frondirion, Dolgellau — a train passes the Cambrian goods warehouse. John Thomas collection. (National Library of Wales).

7 Narrow-gauge Pioneers

THE NARROW-GAUGE LINES which now provide fun for tourists began life in deadly earnest. Most of them served the slate industry, which brought great wealth to a few and early death to many. Like the quarrymen they too went into decline — but iron and steel can be rejuvenated more readily than human flesh, and the silence of the grave persists while the Great Little Trains of Wales chuff happily down their toy tracks to the sea.

One of the best-known, the Festiniog, was also the first. It was opened in 1836, fifteen years after Parliament had given consent to the building of a harbour at Porthmadog following the reclamation of 7,000 acres by the construction of William Maddocks's mile-long Cob. There was little local support for the railway, which came into existence simply because an Irish barrister had too much time on his hands. He was Henry Archer, who happened to meet quarry owner Samuel Holland at a country inn. Archer said he was 'very desirous of doing something', as he had given up legal work and hated being idle. He was thinking of renting the Nantlle Railway, a 3 ft 6 in horse tramway running from the Nantlle Valley to the sea at Caernarfon, but Holland told him he'd be better employed in making a line from Blaenau Ffestiniog to Porthmadog.

Archer must have been a man of mettle. The path from Blaenau to the sea lay through country wilder than any that had yet seen iron rails. Someone easily discouraged would have taken one look at it and decided to leave it to the pack horses — but New Year's Day 1830 found him tramping a possible route with Holland, fired with the dream of railway wagons rolling down from the hills filled with slates bound for the rapidly-growing towns in the Midlands and the North.

A few weeks later the two men called on the engineer James Spooner, who lived at Tan-yr-Allt Isa, near Tremadoc, and had worked with Maddocks on the Cob. They found him in low spirits after the death of his daughter in a shooting accident, all the more tragic for the shot having been fired by his eldest son. Spooner, perhaps because of his depression, thought himself unequal to the task, but he was persuaded to attempt it and Thomas Pritchard was enlisted as foreman. An Act of 1832 gave the Festiniog Railway Company powers to make a railway or tramroad from Porthmadog to slate quarries near Ffestiniog, which would be 'the means of opening a more direct, easy, cheap and commodious communication between the interior of the principal slate and other quarries in the county of Merioneth and the various shipping places'. All the original capital came from Archer's Irish friends.

The railway, nearly 14 miles in length, had a gauge of 1 ft 11 ½ in and was carried at first on stone blocks instead of timber sleepers. It had a gala opening with cannon firing, bands playing and Mr Spooner providing entertainment for the favoured few at his new home, Morfa Lodge. 'I had a short train of waggons loaded with slate and a great number of carriages laden with people,' wrote Holland. '(We) all went up to the inclines in the carriages, drawn by horses, but we all came down without horses, the inclination being sufficient to enable us to do so.' In those early days the line was worked entirely by horses, which had a long haul up to Blaenau but an easy ride back in special Dandy wagons as the trains were brought down by gravity.

The line was beautifully engineered by Spooner, who by means of great loops and slate shelves on the mountain slopes managed to avoid steep gradients in the 700 ft descent. The worst gradient was 1 in 79 which, considering the terrain, was something of a miracle. His anxiety to avoid stiffer tests is understandable when one remembers that at the time there were grave doubts about the ability of a wheel to stay on a smooth track for long descents. James Spooner died in 1856 but his son Charles, who succeeded him as engineer, kept up such a good standard of maintenance that the technical journals of the time called the Festiniog one of the best examples of permanent way to be found anywhere, irrespective of gauge.

Porthmadog grew rapidly after the opening of the railway, and at Blaenau slate production soared. Even in James Spooner's lifetime it had become obvious that the days of horse transport were numbered, but when he suggested steam engines on the line the most eminent railway engineers, including Robert Stephenson, scoffed at the notion. The gauge was too small, they said, for it to be anything but a disaster. They had to eat their words, however, when two engines arrived from George England's Hatcham Ironworks in 1863 at a cost of £1,000 apiece — 'low-built but beautiful little engines', according to a local scribe. These tiny 0-4-0 saddle tanks, weighing only seven tons, were said to be 'equal to the task assigned them', drawing a train with 200 passengers up the line at a speed of 10-12 mph.

It was a 'fine and brilliant day' when this momentous journey took place and an eye-witness, Richard Richards of Bangor, said that hundreds of people who had never seen a steam engine in their lives turned out to watch.

'Horses galloped distraught about the fields when the puffing engines passed along,' he wrote, 'so confused and amazed were they at the noise and the phenomenon altogether; and the more timid cows and sheep seemed equally astonished. All along the line of rails, at every available spot, crowds of wondering people were collected in groups, from the aged crone of ninety years, to the demure little damsel of three. Here and there, the tops of the craggy hills were covered with curious and (dare we say?) gaping crowds of mountaineers, who for the first time in their lives saw a train of carriages propelled up an incline without any horse to draw them ... When the trains arrived at the terminus, at Blaenau Ffestiniog, we were greeted by hundreds of quarrymen, who were perched on the rocks many yards above us, who cheered lustily and uproariously, and as only true Britons can.'

A regular passenger service began in 1865 — itself a landmark in railway history, as until then no line with a gauge less than 4 ft 8½ in had been allowed to carry passengers. Four more engines arrived, including the colourfully-named *Welsh Pony* and *Little Giant*, and the eyes of the world were on the Festiniog. From the moment locomotives appeared on the line it was seen as an example which might fruitfully be followed in India and the Colonies, but it was the introduction of Robert Fairlie's revolutionary 0-4-4-0 *Little Wonder* in 1869 that brought people from far-distant

Fairlies Patent Little Wonder, John Thomas collection.
(National Library of Wales).

countries to this remote part of Wales. Fairlie's double-bogie engine, uniting two boilers on a long frame, brilliantly solved the problem of how to provide more motive power on a narrow-gauge line. To the uninitiated it was something out of comic opera, looking for all the world like two engines stuck back to back with a central cab and a chimney at each end. There was nothing Gilbertian about its performance, however, and its prodigious hauling feats finally nailed the lie that steam was wasted on the narrow gauge. The more exitable converts went to the other extreme, proposing the scrapping of the standard gauge and its replacement by broad gauge on main lines, with narrow gauge branch lines worked by Fairlie locomotives!

In the 1870s the *Little Wonder* proved itself in a long series of tests attended by eminent railway engineers and foreign diplomats, a delegation from the Tsar being headed by Count Alexis Brobinsky, president of the Imperial Russian Commission. As a result railway systems made in the image of Festiniog were adopted in countries as far apart as Mexico and New Zealand, and a grateful Robert Fairlie gave the company free use of his patent in perpetuity.

Meanwhile, another slate line destined for fame as a tourist toy railway in the 20th century had come into existence. The Talyllyn, with its 2 ft 3 in gauge and speed restriction of 15 mph, had opened for traffic in 1866 along six miles of track from Towyn to Abergynolwyn. Right from the start, it was designed for steam locomotion. The remarkable Spooner family who had pioneered the Festiniog had a hand in this enterprise, too, for the engineer was James Swinton Spooner, another of James Spooner senior's talented sons. He had a much easier task than his father had faced, for the terrain was less obdurate and the only major engineering work was a three-span viaduct 52 ft high carrying the line over a ravine at Dolgoch.

The two original 0-4-0 tank engines, *Talyllyn* and *Dolgoch*, were built by Fletcher Jennings and Co. of Whitehaven, and at first they took two trains a day in either direction. As the first narrow gauge line to be promoted as a public carrier both of passengers and goods the railway made history, and even in its earliest days people were alive to its tourist potential. 'No doubt during the summer months extra trains will run for the accommodation of tourists and visitors to enable them to visit the far-famed Tal-y-Llyn Lake, the old Caerberllan Castle, and the ancient church of Llanfihangel, as well as Cader Idris,' wrote a newspaper correspondent.

The engine drivers had to rough it at first, for even in that rainy climate neither locomotive had a cab, nor even a weatherboard. In expecting their employees to display a spartan indifference to cold and damp, however, the Talyllyn were no more inconsiderate than other railway companies of their day. Their passengers did not sit in the lap of luxury either, for the rolling

Father of all narrow gauge railways: Double Fairlie locomotive Merddin Emrys at Tan-y-Bwlch, Festiniog Railway.

stock had no lighting or heating and smoking was forbidden. Such concessions to comfort, indeed, would have astonished the quarrymen who left Towyn on a special train at 6 o'clock every Monday morning to begin their week's labours. There was no going home that night to the comforts of the hearth. Instead they remained all week at the Abergynolwyn quarry of Bryn Eglwys, eating and sleeping in a primitive hostel called The Barracks before returning to Towyn on Friday evening.

One of the first engine drivers on the Talyllyn had the dubious distinction of driving his train over the end of the slate wharf at Towyn, but he appears to have treated the incident with panache. On being sacked, he promptly walked to Machynlleth and was given a job on the Corris Railway, where he remained until his retirement.

The Corris, promoted as a mineral line late in the 1850s, shared Talyllyn's preference for the unusual gauge of 2 ft 3 in. It took slate from the quarries in the Corris area to the Dovey estuary, running six miles from Aberllefenni to Machynlleth. It was a horse-drawn tramway until 1879, when locomotives were introduced for goods traffic, and steam passenger services began four years later. They were an immediate success, for by now railway companies and hoteliers were alive to the commercial possibilities of these quaint little lines climbing through some of the most spectacular countryside in Britain. By the turn of the century the Corris had joined forces with the Cambrian and Talyllyn in promoting a Grand Tour over the metals of all three companies, the only break in the round journey by rail being the distance between the Corris and Talyllyn's railheads of Aberllefenni and Abergynolwyn respectively, which was covered by horse buses. The Grand Tour, which took in the Cambrian's section of main line from Towyn to Machynlleth, was so successful that there was talk of making a railway from Aberllefenni to Abergynolwyn, but the cost proved prohibitive.

The Corris Railway Guide of 1895 struck a picaresque note typical of the times. 'Miniature Gauge, with Bijou Saloon Carriages, starting from Machynlleth, where the Cambrian and Corris Stations adjoin. Real Picturesque Wales. Charming River, Lake and Mountain Scenery, abounding in Glens and Waterfalls . . . From Whit Monday to end of September coaches run twice a day between Corris and Tal-y-Llyn, allowing ample time for ascending Cader Idris. Fares 1/- Single, 1/9 Double Journey.

'This narrow-gauge or "Toy" line runs through one of the most delightful little valleys in Wales; mountain and river and wood blending together most harmoniously, and presenting a succession of charming scenery throughout the whole of the Journey . . . It is reached by taking the Cambrian train to Machynlleth, where you alight and go down the steps to the Corris

The Machynlleth — Corris Railway. John Thomas collection.
(National Library of Wales).

Railway Station and get into the "Toy" train of miniature saloons; although so small it is surprisingly comfortable and travels smoothly. The whistle of the Lilliputian Engine is sounded and away we go . . .'

Cheap day return tickets for combined trips by rail and coach to Talyllyn Lake and Cader Idris were offered 'excursionists' for 8s 9d first class and 5s 9d third class from Oswestry and Whitchurch, and 9s 9d first and 6s 3d third from Pwllheli. The Corris, however, was not invariably popular with its local clientele. In the summer of 1902 the *Cambrian News* reported that the management was reluctant to introduce an extra train in the morning to connect with one from the coast. In a trenchant leading article the editor said the services were 'so bad and so utterly inadequate that it will not be difficult for the people to devise some means of doing without the miserable railway altogether.'

The success of the Festiniog and Talyllyn gave rise to a grandiose scheme for a network of narrow-gauge lines in North Wales, linking Caernarfon with Beddgelert, Betws-y-coed, Corwen and Porthmadog, but very little came of it. The promoters of the North Wales Narrow Gauge Railway — 'quarry owners, landed proprietors and other gentlemen interested in the district concerned' — had to be content with a short line from Dinas, on the LNWR Caernarfon-Afon Wen line, to Rhyd-ddu, three miles short of Beddgelert, with a branch from Tryfan Junction to slate quarries in the neighbourhood of Bryngwyn. Parliamentary powers were granted in 1872 but because of difficulties with the contractor the first trains did not run until 1877, when some of the ironwork on the bridges already needed repainting.

The gauge was 1 ft 11½ in and the names of the stations showed a high-handed disregard for local feeling: the one nearest Llyn Cwellyn was called Quellyn and Rhyd-ddu appeared in the time-table as South Snowdon. There were 47,000 third-class passengers in 1878, mostly quarrymen and other workmen, but a slump in the slate trade meant only half that number the following year and the company never recovered from this unhappy start. Its safety record failed to inspire confidence, either, and many derailments were recorded. One of the most bizarre accidents occurred when the two rear coaches were left behind at Snowdon Ranger, the station between Quellyn and South Snowdon. The engine driver, reversing 600 yards to retrieve them, hit them so hard that they were thrown on their sides. It turned out that the driver, fireman and guard had all been drinking at the Snowdon Ranger Hotel. The guard was drunk but, apparently, 'not so drunk as the driver'.

After the First World War, which saw a wholesale closure of slate quarries, the line was extended to Porthmadog and renamed the Welsh Highland Railway, a title which proved more jaunty than its prospects. There was virtually no freight traffic and the hopes of a lucrative passenger service faded rapidly with the advent of motor buses. The railway was its own worst enemy in some respects, becoming notorious for its poor time-keeping. When a receiver was appointed in 1927 after a petition from Caernarvonshire County Council, which was owed £2,000 interest, the judge

Corris railway station, about 1905. John Thomas collection. (National Library of Wales).

The Countess — *one of the engines built for the opening of the Welshpool and Llanfair Railway in 1903.* (Pronto Photo History).

remarked that the service had never been good. After a wearisome wait, he observed, one might be told there was no train and have to walk. All the same, he added charitably, he was sorry the line had fallen on evil days. Ten years later, all services had ceased.

The railway with the tiniest track of all, the 1ft 3 in gauge Fairbourne, was originally a 2 ft gauge horse-drawn tramway taking building materials from a brickworks towards Penrhyn Point. It was owned by Sir Arthur McDougall, of self-raising flour fame, to whom this little resort on the southern side of the Mawddach estuary virtually owes its existence. As visitors filled the new boarding houses, however, the tramway was acquired in 1916 by a firm which narrowed the gauge and changed to steam traction. The first locomotive, the 4-4-2 tender engine *Prince Edward of Wales*, had 18 in driving wheels and weighed about two tons in running trim.

The Welsh Highland Railway. The terrain was grander than the company's prospects.
(Pronto Photo History).

The Snowdon Mountain Railway, opened in 1896, has the distinction of being the only rack-and-pinion railway in Britain. Pinions on the driving-axles of the locomotive engage with the teeth of a rack laid between the rails, thus giving the grip necessary to surmount gradients of 1 in 5½. The rack principle was first used at the Middleton Colliery in Yorkshire in 1812, but it was an enterprising American who showed its potential for mountain railways half a century later. After spending a miserable night on the 6,293 ft Mount Washington in New Hampshire in appalling weather, he announced his determination to take a railway to the summit. People thought him crazy, but his persistence won the day and the final section was completed in 1869.

The 2 ft 7½ in gauge Snowdon Railway, however, was modelled on the system introduced in Switzerland by Dr Roman Abt, who improved on Niklaus Riggenbach's rack railway up Mount Rigi, opened in 1871. The first sod was cut at the end of 1894, when the whole of Llanberis turned out for the jollifications and 'platoons of rock-cannon' fired salvos in celebration. Taking the line up the mountain proved a test for the toughest of navvies: they worked through the winter in biting winds and rain that chilled to the marrow, living on site in huts and plodding down the mountain at week-ends for a well-earned break. When the railway opened on Easter Monday 1896, however, the high spirits of the management were dashed by a fatal accident. The locomotive, *Ladas*, left the track when coming down from the summit, hurtled over the edge of a precipice and was dashed to pieces. The coaches, which were equipped with brakes, were brought to a halt but in the meantime two passengers had panicked and leapt from the train, one of

Train at Llanberis on the Snowdon Mountain Railway in 1898.
(National Library of Wales).

them, the landlord of the Padarn Villa Hotel, Llanberis, dying of his injuries. The railway closed immediately, not to be reopened till the following year. It was an instant success, with over 12,000 passengers in its first full season.

As the century drew to a close, two more narrow-gauge lines were promoted: the Vale of Rheidol Light Railway from Aberystwyth to Devil's Bridge, and the Welshpool and Llanfair Light Railway from Welshpool to Llanfair Caereinion. The latter, which became known as the farmers' line, was built to the unusual gauge of 2 ft 6 in and was operated from the start by Cambrian Railways. The original locomotives were identical Beyer, Peacock 0-6-0 side tanks, *The Earl* and *The Countess*, which were later equipped with larger cabs and new boilers by the GWR. *The Countess*, decked with green and red muslin, red rosettes and daffodils, drew the ceremonial train on opening day in April 1903, when jugfuls of champagne were handed out by an enthusiastic innkeeper. Trains on market day were crammed with farmers' wives clutching baskets of eggs and butter, but passenger services as a whole never lived up to expectations and ceased — though not finally — in 1931.

A line up the Vale of Rheidol was originally conceived by the Manchester and Milford Railway as a branch from its proposed station at Devil's Bridge, but nothing came of this and it was many years before the idea was revived. The railway was promoted in 1896 with the twin purpose of taking lead from the mines in the Rheidol Valley to the sea and cashing in on the tourist traffic. The owner of Green's Foundry in Aberystwyth, who owned the

Rheidol Mines near Devil's Bridge, suggested running the line along the floor of the valley but it was decided to hug the hillside in the way originally proposed by the M and M.

One of the directors was Montague Smith, well-known at the time as a promoter of London's first Tube railways, and the contractors were the Pethick brothers of Plymouth, who built the Vauxhall and London bridges. Sir James Szlumper was appointed engineer, a decision which won local approval as he had previously engineered the M and M line from Pencader to Aberystwyth. Progress was slow at first due to a shortage of labour but this problem was solved with the completion of the Elan Valley reservoir project and an influx of navvies looking for work. Some of them did not stay long when they found there were no pubs in the vicinity, but the formation of drinking clubs overcame the crisis.

The first two locomotives, *Edward VII* and *Prince of Wales*, were 2-6-2 tank engines made by Davies and Metcalfe of Romiley, near Stockport, the *Cambrian News* noting that Mr Metcalfe 'formerly resided at Aberystwyth, where he invented an injector which is now in use all over the world where locomotives are employed'. The line was regarded as a perfect example of narrow gauge engineering, rising 480 ft in just over four miles beyond Aberffrwd at 1 in 50 to reach a height of 680 ft at Devil's Bridge at the end of the 12-mile journey. The breathtaking views of the wooded gorge came as a surprise even to the Aberystwyth people who went on the early trains, for

The Rheidol locomotive on the Vale of Rheidol Railway. (Arthur Lewis collection, National Library of Wales).

they had never seen the valley thus before. The precipitous drop to the left in the final stages of the journey made even strong men flinch: on the trial trip in August 1902, one passenger was said to have refused to make the return journey, saying he would rather walk. No such theatricals were reported by the *Cambrian News* in its account of the official opening run three months later, when 'everyone present was charmed with the magnificent views which continually opened out as the train sped onward and upward'. There was loud acclaim for Ald. E. P. Wynne, a former mayor of Aberystwyth, when he declared that they had heard a great deal about the Corris and Festiniog lines, but these were now eclipsed by the Vale of Rheidol. Another speaker, Major Price Lewes, said he had travelled the world and 'did not know where he had seen, from first to last, a more beautiful piece of scenery'.

When the lead mines closed, the beauty of the valley remained. We shall see, in a later chapter, how the Vale of Rheidol and narrow-gauge lines elsewhere took on a new lease of life in the post-war era.

En route for Devil's Bridge.
(Arthur Lewis collection,
National Library of Wales).

~ EN ROUTE FOR DEVIL'S BRIDGE ~

8 The Severn Tunnel

IN DECEMBER 1879, one of the world's best-known railway contractors made his way to the muddy shores of the Severn Estuary near Port-skewett, five miles west of Chepstow. He was Thomas Walker, who had made railways in Canada, Russia, Egypt and the Sudan. He had overcome many obstacles in the past, but this time he faced the most daunting task of all: the construction of the Severn Tunnel.

The size of the job was, by then, obvious not only to the imagination but to the naked eye. The work had already been in progress six years, with little to show for it. Shafts had been sunk on either side of the estuary and headings driven, but two months before Walker's arrival on the scene all the workings connected with the Old Shaft had been flooded by a flow of fresh spring water which quickly overpowered the pumps. The men had raced to safety, pursued by a swirling flood that rose above their knees and quickly filled the shaft. With 350,000 gallons an hour pouring into the workings the people living around found all their wells suddenly run dry, with the result that for two days they were hard put to meet their basic requirements.

The calamity convinced the directors of the GWR that they needed to tackle the job in a more full-blooded way. On the advice of their consulting engineer, Sir John Hawkshaw, they accepted Walker's tender for £948,959, having first rejected it as too high two years previously. He arrived to find a dispiriting scene:

'Nothing could be more desolate than the appearance of the works at this time. There were near the main shaft only six cottages and a small office, the necessary boiler-houses and engine-houses, a small carpenter's shop, a fitter's shop, a blacksmith's shop, and two low buildings or sheds, used as cottages also . . . The engines of the main shaft stood idle, the boilers were out of steam, most of the men who had been employed had left in search of other work, and the water in the shaft was standing up to the level of high water in the Severn.'

Walker buckled down to the task without delay. He ordered larger pumps and began sinking four new shafts. He also decided that the tunnel should be further beneath the river bed than originally planned. The intention had been to run the railway 50 feet below the rocky bottom of The Shoots, the deep channel through which the current runs at low water, but he thought an extra 15 feet was required. This meant deepening all the shafts and a slight alteration of the gradient on the Monmouthshire side, making it 1 in 90 instead of 1 in 100. He was surprised to find that the lesson of the flooding had not been learned: 'Even after this irruption of the water under the land,' he wrote, 'no one seemed to be fully alive to the fact that the greatest dangers and difficulties were to be found there, but everyone still thought the danger lay in the construction of the tunnel in the deepest part of the river.'

In their headlong flight for safety the men had left open an iron door underground which it was essential to close before much progress could be made. A diver had to be found willing to grope his way in total darkness along the flooded heading for 340 yards, a task made immeasurably more difficult by the fact that he would stumble over skips, beams, tools and other debris. Only a hero would attempt it, but one was found in a diver of great experience named Lambert. With two divers behind him passing his air hose forward he set out on his perilous journey, but within 30 yards of the door he had to return. He made two further attempts before acknowledging defeat, the trouble being that in spite of the help of his colleagues the hose was impossible to manage. Plainly, some other method had to be found. Walker promptly sent a telegram to Fleuss, the inventor of a new apparatus enabling a diver to dispense with an air pipe by carrying a knapsack of compressed air. Fleuss arrived full of confidence and descended the shaft with Lambert, who was to see him on his way and give him much-needed encouragement. After three attempts, however, Fleuss gave up, saying he would not close that door for £1,000. Only Lambert could save the day now, but he had never worn the new gear and did not much relish it. Walker's persuasive tongue, however, and his own professional pride, made him reluctantly agree to experiment. After spending half an hour under the water in the strange outfit, he declared himself willing to venture into the heading again.

Walker's delight gave way to apprehension as the moment drew near. Was he about to send a brave man to his death? He urged Lambert to beware his knapsack did not strike the roof of the heading or any timbers that might fracture the small copper pipe which took the air to his helmet. Lambert nodded impatiently. He had a job to do, and had steeled himself for it. He reached the door at his first attempt in the Fleuss gear and removed some rails blocking the way, but could not complete the task. After a day's rest he again walked the flooded passage and this time succeeded in closing the heavy door and shutting a sluice valve. When he triumphantly broke surface after an hour and a quarter, Walker was surprised to find that he showed no signs of exhaustion.

By December 7, 1880, the works were clear of water and Walker pressed ahead with the tunnelling. His first step was to build a strong wall in the westward heading from the Old Shaft to keep the Great Spring which had caused all the trouble at bay. He was also active in providing accommodation for the workers, and by this time there was a sizeable community at Sudbrook. The foremen had semi-detached homes which were a cut above the terraces housing married couples and lodgers, while the principal foreman, Joseph Talbot, had a still more substantial home for his family. A mission hall was supplied with preachers by the Evangelization Society and services were held on Sundays and Wednesdays. There was a day school and Sunday school, and a new road had been made from the shaft to the nearest public road by the Black Rock Hotel, enabling tradesmen from Chepstow and Caldicot to bring their goods to the site. In the spring of 1881, however, Walker had a strike on his hands.

Trouble had threatened for some time. In his own story of the undertaking, *The Severn Tunnel: Its Construction and Difficulties,* he admits that 'The men who had been working for six years for the Great Western Railway Company before the contract was let to me had always felt a grudge against me, perhaps because they had had easier times under the old regime.' Walker had certainly made demanding work more arduous still. He had replaced eight-hour shifts with ten-hour shifts which meant that, with an hour for breakfast at 9 a.m. and an hour for dinner at 1 o'clock, the men started work at six in the morning and knocked off at six at night. The story of the strike is best told in Walker's own words, which show clearly the attitude of a Victorian employer who, while anxious to attend to the material and spiritual needs of his employees, was ruthless in dealing with any hint of rebellion.

'There had been a bad spirit among the men from the time I had taken possession of the works. I believe they had wished that I should fail in pumping the water out of the tunnel. I am not quite sure that they had not wilfully caused some of the difficulties that had occurred; and now that the works were opened throughout, and there was a prospect of making better progress, they determined to make a stand, and either force me to abandon the work altogether, or yield to their demands.

'Their discontent first showed itself by their jeering at the men who took their meals with them up the long heading, asking them why they did not get tin hats made to carry their dinners in, and then by assaulting them in the darkness, or when they could meet with them alone, men I had brought from a tunnel I had just finished at Dover.

'At last, on Saturday 21st May (1881), a notice appeared, written in chalk, at the top of the main shaft: "I hope the — bond will break, and kill any man that goes down to work." The men gathered round the pit, but refused to go below . . . After refusing to commence the shift they went off to the nearest public house, came back primed with drink, and gathered in front of the pay-office grumbling; but they never came to me or the foreman and stated any grievance or asked for any concession. They simply determined to make trouble and stop the works if they could. I was in the office at the time, so I went down into the middle of them and said:

'Now, what do you fellows want?'

'No answer.

'Now, tell me what you want, and stop hanging about here.'

'Then one of them said: "We wants the eight-hour shifts."

'I said: "My good man, you will never get that if you stop here for a hundred years. There's a train at 2 o'clock and if you don't make haste and get your money you'll lose your train. You had better get your money as soon as you can, and go."

'The men looked very sheepish, went to the pay-office and got their money, and the works were absolutely deserted for the following four days . . . It was a good thing for the works that this strike occurred when it did, for it cleared away a number of bad characters who had gathered on the works; and from this time to the completion of the contract there was hardly any trouble with the men and I think there was a thoroughly good feeling between the employer and employed.'

By the end of September 1881 the two headings were joined up under the river and through ventilation was established by a fan at Sudbrook instead of compressed air. A number of explosives had been employed, including dynamite, gelatine, tonite and gun-cotton, and by the spring of the following year there was even electric light — then in its infancy — at either end of the tunnel. There were large cabins alongside each shaft where the men could eat and dry their clothes, and the life of the community had been enhanced by the provision of a coffee house and reading room, and a schoolroom with a certificated master. In the summer of 1882 an infirmary was opened in Sudbrook with a resident doctor, matron, sister and assistant nurse, who treated not only the men employed on the works but their families, too. There were over 3,000 on the pay-roll then but, says Walker, 'considering the magnitude of the undertaking, the difficulties encountered and the number of men employed night and day, we were very free from accidents during the six years the works were in progress . . . The principal illness that the men suffered from was pneumonia, caused no doubt by the great heat and damp below, and by the careless exposure when they came out of the works'. Walker's enthusiasm for the moral welfare of the families under his wing is strikingly illustrated by the fact that within three weeks of the mission room burning to the ground, a new one twice the size was opened.

There was a nasty moment at the end of 1882 when, one Sunday night,

Walker heard panic-stricken cries of "The water's in!" Breathlessly, a group of workmen told him that hundreds had fled in terror but as they could give no clear picture of events he was able to maintain an air of icy calm as he informed them he would promptly investigate. In the tunnel, he found to his relief that a false alarm had been raised. Between 300 and 400 men had fled shouting and screaming from an imaginery horror, discarding clothing as they ran. Hats, neckerchiefs, leggings and waistcoats had been precipitately cast away — but while their comrades jeered when the truth were known, Walker was inclined to be charitable.

'It would be wrong for anyone to blame the men for cowardice,' he wrote. 'I am sure that a finer body of men could not be found in England. They were men who had had a thoroughly hard training and accustomed as they were to work in dangerous positions, and knowing every time they went below that each man took his life in his hand, they still went cheerfully to their work, and were no doubt as brave as Englishmen always are. But to understand how easily a panic spreads, under the circumstances, it would be necessary one's self to be under the river, a mile away from the shaft, confined in a narrow space with rocks dripping or running with water all round, with only the light of a stray candle here and there, and the most extraordinary sounds that ever greeted the ears of mortal man; first from the east, and then from the west, heavy timbers thrown down suddenly, with a noise that re-echoed through the whole of the works; then a stray shot fired in one direction, then a complete salvo of 50 or 60 shots from the other — every sound totally different from the sounds in the open air — all the surroundings such as must produce a feeling of awe and tension of the nerves . . .'

October, 1883, however, brought real disaster. The Great Spring burst in again, 'rolling up all at once like a great horse', in the graphic words of a ganger. Men and iron skips were alike swept away but, miraculously, there was no loss of human life. Three ponies died, however, and five were rescued by men wading waist deep. The lower part of the tunnel was soon flooded and although the pumps were kept going at full speed the water rose at the rate of four feet an hour. The flood extended for a mile and a half and was halted on the Bristol side by a hastily-built brick wall. A week later, on a stormy night with a high tide running, a tidal wave swept over the low-lying ground between the Marsh Shaft and the river on the Welsh side of the works. The wall of water, six feet high, smashed into the workmen's cottages at Sudbrook and roared down the Marsh Shaft, where 83 men were at work on the night shift. Some escaped up ladders but one man, John Bartlett — known as Fighting Barney — lost his grip 'as if exhausted' and fell to his death. The trapped men retreated up the gradient towards the west end of the section of tunnel they were building, but their prospects looked grim as the water rose to within eight feet of the roof. They sang and prayed in the darkness, while on the surface their comrades threw together sacking, timber and waterproof clothing to dam the tide. Planks were hopefully lowered so that rafts might be made, but the only practical means of escape was by boat. At last one was brought down the shaft by wire rope, but there were still obstacles to overcome. The way was blocked by timbers, and the rescuers had to turn back for a cross-cut saw. Eventually, however, the men were brought out five or six at a time.

Walker's pumps did their job so effectively that the works were cleared of water surprisingly quickly, and the tidal wave proved to be nature's last assault on the tunnel. By the end of 1884 it was virtually complete, and in April 1885 the last of the 76,400 million bricks used in its construction was laid. Nearly four and a half miles long, the tunnel had taken its place among the engineering marvels of the Victorian age. When the first train ran through on September 5, 1885 — a 'special' for high-ranking officials of the GWR — the *South Wales Daily News* said it had been a 'memorable year' which had also seen the opening of the Mersey Tunnel. Comparisons were drawn with the tunnels through the Alps, which were greater in scale but, the paper thought, easier to engineer than work 'under an arm of the sea'. Its report continued:

Locomotive emerging from Severn Tunnel into Wales. (Pronto Photo History).

'The great Swiss tunnels were driven through solid rock, which was drilled away by machinery. The Severn Tunnel has been cut through sandstone, alluvial gravel, and marl, and it may almost be said through underground reservoirs of spring water. Its success seems to prove that, given a necessary amount of money, scarcely any great work is impossible to the skill and perseverance of modern engineers.'

The tunnel, 12 years in the making, had a total cost — including rails — of £1,806,248, and the largest number of men employed at any one time was 3,628. The average pay of miners engaged on the work was £1 18s a week and of labourers £1 7s 6d. Walker, in compiling a statistical record of the project, reckoned that at one time enough water was being pumped away every day to supply a town the size of Liverpool or Manchester.

The first freight train ran through the tunnel on January 9, 1886, and passenger services were introduced before the year was out. They made as radical an improvement in rail travel between South Wales and the West of England as the Severn Bridge was to make in road travel eighty years later. Before the opening of the tunnel people had to take a train from Cardiff to Portskewett, transfer to the New Passage ferry and catch another train to Bristol on the far side of the estuary, a journey of two and a half hours. By 1891, it was taking only 75 minutes to go from Cardiff to Bristol by train through the Severn Tunnel.

The *South Wales Daily News* found a colourful way of describing this new link between South Wales and the West. It was 'the opening of a door hitherto shut between two great commercial peoples.'

9 Barry's 'Marauders'

A S THE SEVERN TUNNEL finally took shape, a Bill went through
Parliament which was to give Wales one of the most energetic of its
railway companies. The Barry Railway came late in the day, enjoying only three decades as an independent company before having its identity
sunk into that of the GWR under the Railways Act of 1921. In that time,
however, its insatiable ambition won it admiration on the one hand and im-
placable hostility on the other. During the most protracted of its battles for
expansion it was called 'sordid and greedy', the 'spoiled child of Parliament'
and 'a marauding company'. One barrister went so far as to suggest an
alliance with the Devil himself. 'It is not a question of Heaven knows where
the Barry will stop,' said Balfour Browne, K.C. 'Only the other place knows.'

The creation of the Barry showed once again the vigour and truculence of
David Davies, by now a Liberal M.P. and one of the richest men in Wales.
Like his fellow coal owners, he was impatient with the inadequate facilities
for shipping coal at Cardiff docks. The port had grown, but not fast enough.
Berths were so scarce that vessels queued up for days, and the legend persists
that when the port was at its busiest it was possible to go from one side of the
docks to the other without setting foot on land: skipping from deck to deck
of the closely-packed ships was enough. The rapid growth of coal production in the Rhondda had also caused severe congestion on the Taff Vale
Railway, and trains laden with black diamonds from Davies's Ocean
collieries were subject to such delays that only drivers of philosophic
temperament were able to endure the frustration of it all. Amazingly, coal
trains from the Rhondda were known to take 23 hours to reach Cardiff.

The last straw for the coal owners was the Bute trustees' decision in 1882
to build the long-awaited Roath Dock, but only at a price — this being an
extra penny a ton on coal shipped from Cardiff. The only escape from the
thraldom of the trustees and the TVR, they decided, was to build an entirely
new port with its own railway system. 'We have five million tons of coal,'

declared David Davies, 'and can fill a thundering good dock the first day we open it.' Ogmore was regarded as a possible site, but in the end the freighters opted for Barry, an insignificant hamlet which had once been notorious as a smugglers' haunt. The first attempt at promoting a Bill failed through the combined opposition of the Bute trustees, the TVR, the Rhymney Railway and other vested interests, but after a long contest in the next Parliamentary session the royal assent was received.

The first sod was ceremonially cut in 1884 by the company chairman, Lord Windsor, who was later created Earl of Plymouth, and Davies could not resist the temptation to show off a little. 'That's not the way, my lord. Let me show you,' he said patronisingly after watching his lordship clumsily turn a piece of turf with a spade of polished oak, and filling the barrow with a flourish he wheeled it triumphantly away. His speech at the banquet that evening set the tone for the Barry's militant approach. 'If the Taff Vale run us down,' he said, 'we will run down the Taff Vale.' The *Western Mail*, however, took a sceptical view of the company's prospects. 'Unless trade goes on increasing,' it declared, 'it will be a poor look out for the new venture.'

Others, however, were not so easily deceived. They saw that in owning the docks as well as the railway, the Barry had an advantage enjoyed by none of its competitors. The Taff Vale responded by attempting to acquire Cardiff docks from the Bute trustees, but while their hopes were high initially they came to nothing. They had to stand helplessly by as the new line was taken nearly 19 miles from Barry to Trehafod in the Rhondda, knowing that a significant part of their coal trade would now be siphoned off by this upstart. Difficult gradients were avoided by some skilful engineering which involved tunnels at Treforest (Pontypridd) and Wenvoe, the latter over a mile long. In July 1889 the new dock in Barry, covering 73 acres, was officially opened, and by that time the sparsely-populated parish had grown in five years into a town of 10,000, with ten chapels in Cadoxton alone. James Szlumper, who engineered the northern part of the railway, said it had been a difficult task, 'and the lawyers in the upper part of the valley had not made it any easier,' he wryly added.

The creation of the port of Barry was yet another personal triumph for David Davies. The running battle he had prophesied began when the Taff Vale reduced their freight charges with the help of a subsidy from the Marquess of Bute, and the Barry were obliged to cut theirs. 'Hang on to your shares for all you are worth,' he grimly told the shareholders. 'Don't be afraid the Taff and Bute people will run us to the ground. They'll run themselves to the ground first." It was to be a 30-year war, resolved only by the absorption of both companies into the GWR, but Davies was to see little of it. Twelve months after that ceremonial opening, he died at the age of 71. At the half-yearly meeting of shareholders at the Park Hotel, Cardiff, in August 1890,

A Barry Railway steam coach of 1905 with, inset, a Barry 120, Class K.

Lord Windsor spoke of the 'irreparable loss' sustained by the company, and it was resolved to erect a 'suitable bronze statue' of the great man in Barry. A more immediate memorial to his acumen, however, was the declaration of a 10 per cent dividend, which firmly set the trend for years ahead.

The Barry Railway's success was achieved in spite of the fact that it had direct access to scarcely a single colliery. It was a buccaneer of a railway, shamelessly raiding the territory of others. It drew its coal traffic from the TVR, the Rhymney, the B and M and the mighty GWR. Nothing deterred these bold adventurers, least of all the natural hazards they encountered. They flung the 1,548 ft Walnut Tree Viaduct across the Nantgarw Gap at Taffs Well to reach the Rhymney Railway's junction near Caerphilly, and a few years later built the even more ambitious Llanbradach Viaduct to tap the B and M's traffic. Costing a quarter of a million pounds, it was among the finest bridges in South Wales, 2,400 ft long and with eleven lattice steel girders on brick piers carrying the line 125 ft above the River Rhymney. Plans for a further extension east into Monmouthshire, however, were thwarted by an alliance of eight rival companies plus Newport Corporation. Feelings ran so high that a public meeting in Caerphilly ended in uproar with the throwing of stink bombs.

To the west, there was less controversial expansion. Colliery owners in the Llynfi, Garw and Ogmore valleys saw the new port of Barry as the kind of spacious and well-equipped dock they so desperately needed, and lost no time in promoting the Vale of Glamorgan Railway. It ran from Tondu to Barry via Bridgend, Aberthaw and Llantwit Major and proved costly to build because of the cuttings required in this limestone country. The last section entailed heavy engineering work, with two short tunnels in Porthkerry Park and the 13-arch Porthkerry viaduct. No sooner was the viaduct opened than it was closed again for repairs to a pier due to subsidence, and for a while passengers were taken from Barry to Rhoose in a horse-drawn brake.

Barry quickly became one of the finest coal ports in the United Kingdom, dealing with as many as 4,000 ships a year. In the boom year of 1913, when steam coal from the Welsh valleys kept the world's navies afloat, it accounted for nearly one-third of the 37 million tons of coal and coke exported from South Wales. But while the mineral traffic made a mint of money for the shareholders, it was not allowed to dominate the railway's affairs to the exclusion of everything else. Passengers were well catered for from the very first day, and before the First World War put an end to the fun and games the company carried up to 50,000 passengers to Barry Island on bank holidays. They were able to do so only by borrowing rolling stock from the GWR, B and M and Rhymney, the motley appearance of these trains contrasting oddly with the Barry's customary spruceness. In Edwardian times the search for perfection was such that the chief mechanical engineer,

A Barry Railway passenger tank engine of 1892.

Henry Frederick Golding, used to order a newly-painted engine back to the paint shop if he found the slightest blemish.

The Barry had the distinction of running the first main line 0-8-0 tender engines in Britain, which were put into service in 1889. Built by Sharp, Stewart and Co, they were originally intended for railways in Scandinavia. The first decade of the 20th century saw the company still pursuing improvement relentlessly. Two steam railcars were introduced on suburban services in 1905, seating ten first-class and 40 third-class passengers, and it is diverting to think of their contrasting clientele: the grey-suited respectability of the commuting office workers, and the noisy exuberance of the day trippers at holiday weekends. They were augmented in 1909 by two auto-trains, which were a cunning means of providing more passenger services without more rolling stock or extra track. They had only one locomotive but could be driven from either end, as the rear coach was equipped with controls. When the railway became part of the Great Western system in the 1920s it had 148 locomotives on its books, four of which were 0-8-0 tender engines and the rest tank engines, 72 of them 0-6-2s and 38 0-6-0s.

The men were as tough and enduring as the machines. There was Bill Dunn, who at the age of 90 was still able to recall how he learned the art of firing an engine from his father. 'If I didn't shove the coal in right he used to give me a clout and a kick up the backside,' he said. 'He learned me with his toe — and one across the ear for remembrance.'

Another veteran, Jack Perrett of Creigiau, had his first job on the railway opening the tollgate between Dinas Powis and Sully; the charge was sixpence a horse and trap. Some of the navvies who built the Barry had worked on the Severn Tunnel before that. 'They had plenty of fights. They used to drink pretty heavy. They had their own shebeen but the police never caught them.'

The line went through the sleepy villages of St George's and Creigiau on its way to the Rhondda. A former signalman at The Drope, St George's, remembered the days when 120 trains a day used to pass his signal box.

The Barry was as stern an employer as other companies at the time, but the men made their own fun. One Derby Day a driver chalked the name of a runner on his engine, tied a rope around the stack and sat on top like a jockey! The engine, one need scarcely add, was not in motion at the time . . .

The Barry Railway was involved, if only obliquely, in the strange decision which the general manager of the Taff Vale Railway had to make on the tricky question of 'diarrhoea mixture' in 1892. Ammon Beasley, who had just taken up his appointment after service with the GWR, found the TVR was issuing this mixture to the men as a matter of course. He was puzzled and not a trifle displeased. 'As I find this is not so in the case of the GWR Company nor the Rhymney and Barry Companies, I do not see why we should continue to supply such medicine in future,' he peremptorily informed the engineer, J. W. Brewer. 'Kindly note.'

10 Disaster!

RAIL TRAVEL, in its early days, had to overcome the same kind of anxieties as those induced by air travel in later times. It was not only the congenitally nervous who blanched at the prospect of being whisked along at the terrifying speed of thirty or forty miles an hour: brave men, too, thought twice about putting themselves at the mercy of a hissing monster which might blow them to atoms any second. The hazards of the journey were too awesome to dwell upon: viaducts spanning dreadful heights, noisome tunnels in the bowels of the earth. Gradually the fears subsided, and people boarded a train as unthinkingly as their grandfathers had stepped onto the stage coach, but from time to time accidents occurred which served as a reminder that, however strict the precautions, railways could never be entirely free from danger.

The Abergele disaster of 1868 was not only one of the worst on record at the time, but peculiarly horrible in that its victims were consumed by a fire so intense that the remains of some of them could scarcely be identified as human. It occurred just before one o'clock on an August afternoon when the Holyhead Mail collided with some runaway trucks filled with casks of paraffin. Thirty-three people perished in the flames and the newspapers dwelt on the grisly details. 'In several cases,' reported *The Times,* 'even cinders of the bones have not been left. What were human forms had been gathered up like so much black dust.'

The cause of the tragedy was the presence on the line ahead of a goods train with two wagons at the rear containing nearly eight tons of paraffin. It arrived at Abergele at 12.15 p.m., nineteen minutes before the mail was due, and was allowed to go on to Llanddulas. There was no room for the whole train in either siding, however, as much of the space was already occupied by wagons. Although time was short, it would still have been possible to shunt the goods into the sidings in two stages, but the Llanddulas stationmaster chose to follow a course of colossal folly. With the mail running only fifteen minutes behind the goods, he decided to carry out some shunting on the main line. The plan was to shunt three timber wagons on to the six rear wagons and brake van left on the main line, couple them up and take them into a siding clear of the mail. The timber wagons were fly-shunted towards the seven standing vehicles, which were on a down gradient of 1 in 147 and secured only by the van brake. They were sent at injudicious speed and hit the trucks with some force, snapping the cog wheel on the van brake.

The scenario for disaster was now complete. The trucks rumbled down the track towards Abergele, with the senior brakesman in hopeless pursuit. When the horrified driver of the mail saw them coming, he shut off the steam and applied the brakes — but a collision was inevitable. 'For God's sake, Joe, jump!' he cried — and hurled himself from the footplate. The fireman, however, stayed put. Driver Holmes heard him utter a cry as the tender went right over the engine on impact.

The paraffin casks burst and instantly the front of the mail — which contained many wealthy people making for the Holyhead ferry to Ireland — was enveloped in flames. There was a vain attempt to put out the fire by workmen from a nearby quarry and other local people, who formed a chain across the sands and filled buckets with sea water. The only survivors, however, were in the rear part of the train. Passengers in the first four coaches perished.

The task of identifying the dead proved grisly and unrewarding. Lord and

The Abergele disaster.
(Illustrated London News).

Lady Farnham were known by their crested watches; those of humbler birth left nothing of themselves. The remains were numbered and described with clinical brevity. One anonymous victim went on record as 'No. 13. Charred remains. Sex unknown . . .' Another as 'No. 16. Human remains; sex unknown; part of skull and thorax, with part of vertebrae.' *The Times* observed that the ashes of the dead were 'not distinguishable from the charcoal dust of the carriages.' The bodies were placed in a mass grave 'side by side without any distinction of rank, without any difference in the coffins that enclose them.' And the heart-searching began.

On the morning after a catastrophe 'unparalleled in our English experience', *The Times* had raised the question 'whether any train should be allowed to pass through a station until the line between it and the next station is known to be clear.' Two days later — a Sunday intervened — its leader writer wondered 'whether, indeed, it has been usual to handle petroleum with too much confidence.' In future 'no railway company, we may be confident, will carry such an article again except under the strictest precautions.' There were letters from readers within a few days of the tragedy. One correspondent said the telegraph was not in use on the line 'although the traffic at this season of the year is very great, and almost all the trains are very irregular.'

The *Liverpool Daily Post* carried a leading article, too. Headlined 'The Way to Prevent Railway Accidents', it said that 'railroads' were 'unequal to the duty they have to perform. There is not railway room enough.' Railways had been opposed by land owners, who had forced companies to pay high prices for the land they acquired. 'Railway companies, therefore, appropriated to their use as little land as possible.' Thus the presence of the mail and the goods on the same rails. (The culpability of the Llanddulas stationmaster was not then obvious, and in any event did not detract from the main argument.) 'The roads — at least, all the great roads — of traffic must be widened in order that more rails may be laid down.'

Colonel Rich of the Board of Trade held the stationmaster responsible for the improper shunting, censured the senior brakesman for not securing the wagons firmly, criticised the time-table and called for the block telegraph to be installed between Abergele and Llanddulas. Railway companies, he observed, allowed many of their safety rules to be broken daily, and staff often neglected their duties. The result was that trains were frequently late. If the train had left Abergele on time the collision would have occurred just outside Llanddulas, where the trucks would have been moving more slowly and the paraffin casks might not have broken.

The Abergele disaster — the worst in Welsh rail history — haunted the popular imagination for years to come, and the obvious flaws which it revealed in railway practice led to stricter precautions generally. The accident on the Friog decline in Merioneth in 1883 made an impression for quite a different reason. There were only two fatalities, but there could have been many more. Only a lucky chance — or the hand of Providence — saved a whole train plunging over a cliff, and people soberly reflected on the risks inherent in a journey through mountainous country on a wild winter's night. The accident occurred on a section of Cambrian line north of Llwyngwril which had been notoriously difficult to engineer. The track followed a ledge above the rock-strewn shore at a lower level than the turnpike road which had terrified stage coach travellers, many of whom had decided to walk rather than risk riding so near a precipice. The road was supported by a retaining wall, an embankment of shale and rock separating it from the railway. After days of heavy rain part of this wall gave way, and tons of debris fell on to the track. The evening train from Machynlleth on New Year's Day ploughed into it and the engine and tender plunged 60 ft to the rocks, killing the driver and fireman — both named William Davies, and both from Porthmadog. The lives of the passengers were saved only because the couplings between the tender and coaches snapped. The first carriage was suspended over the cliff, the second overturned and the third, which contained most of the passengers, stayed on the rails. When news of the accident reached Dolgellau it was believed at first that the whole train had fallen into the sea, and a disaster such as the Tay Bridge was feared. The annual eisteddfod was brought to an early close and two doctors, Hugh Jones and Edward Jones, hurried to the scene. Although it was after midnight when they returned, they found a crowd of people on the platform at Dolgellau awaiting them. At the inquest, guard Richard Newell said the train had not been going faster than the regulation four miles an hour for this perilous stretch of line, and the coroner thought it 'a most miraculous thing that the coupling between the tender and the train broke.' Were it not for this, he added soberly, the accident would have been fearful. The jury returned verdicts of accidental death and considered the cutting unsafe. The *Cambrian News* said the coast line 'from the tunnels and sharp curves at Aberdovey to Harlech cutting' had always been a source of anxiety and expense to the Cambrian company, and workmen were 'almost continually engaged in and about the Friog cutting'.

In South Wales, the pell-mell progress of a locomotive in the early hours of a Sunday morning in 1871 was reported in the *Western Mail* under the headline, 'Remarkable Exploits of a Runaway Engine at Newport.' The Great Western tank engine No 1032, pushing a van, careered nine miles from Pontypool Road through Newport before coming to a halt near the entrance to Tredegar Park. Its bizarre journey began when the young fireman leapt off the footplate of the stationary engine in a panic after the driver, who was beside the track, shouted 'Look out!' on seeing a Taff Vale engine shunting four wagons coming dangerously close. Unhappily, in his haste to be gone the fireman knocked the regulator open and, after receiving a bump in the rear, No 1032 charged furiously along the line to the amazement of the few people who were up and about. It demolished seventeen sets of level crossing gates, mostly in the populous parts of Newport. 'Some of the gates, which are made of wood, are broken into splinters, and the iron gates are twisted like pieces of wire,' reported the *Western Mail*. 'Happily no lives have been sacrificed.'

Seven years later, 12 people were killed and over 30 injured in a collision on the Rhondda branch of the Taff Vale, about half a mile above Pontypridd station. The only hospital in the town was attached to the workhouse, where the gruesome scene was described in detail in newspaper reports. Medical men in shirtsleeves fought to save the lives of the casualties, whose screams were heart-rending. 'Two cases of amputations of the legs were taking place in the room, and that, for some unexplained reason, without the aid of chloroform . . . The hospital was a veritable shambles, and was quite enough to unnerve the stoutest heart,' wrote the *Western Mail's* man on the spot. The paper indignantly called attention to Pontypridd's want of a public hospital or infirmary. 'In the centre of a district teeming with a vast mining population, it's a glaring anomaly that there could exist no public institution to which on occasions of this sort sufferers may be conveyed. Treated at their homes or in public houses the men injured by the pit accidents which from time to time take place are not infrequently done to death by the mistaken kindness of their relatives.' At the inquest signalman William Roberts, who had been with the TVR for over 30 years, was found guilty of gross neglect by the coroner, and the jury returned a verdict of manslaughter.

Two more disasters occurred on the Taff Vale before the First World War. In 1893, one of the under-hung springs of a 4-4-2 tank engine snapped after the link holding it gave way and six coaches ran down an embankment at Llantrisant, killing 13 passengers. The other accident occurred at Hopkinstown, just outside Pontypridd, when a passenger train crashed into the rear of a slowly-moving mineral train in broad daylight. Four carriages were splintered into matchwood and 11 people were killed, including three miners' leaders. The tragedy was attributed to a 'misunderstanding in signalling.'

The accident at Abermule in January 1921 ranked with the Abergele disaster in its impact on the public. Two trains collided on a stretch of single track between Newtown and Abermule, and 17 people were killed and 36 injured. Like the Abergele tragedy, it was the result of human folly. The rules for single-line working on the electric tablet system were flagrantly breached, not just by one man but by several. In the words of the coroner at the inquest, 'If there were spirits of carelessness and irresponsibility, they must have been over Abermule on that fateful day.'

The collision was between the 10.25 a.m. express from Aberystwyth to

Manchester and the 10.05 stopping train from Whitchurch to Aberystwyth. They met on a curve a mile from Abermule station, where they should have safely passed each other. 'We saw the other train as we rounded the bend,' said John Owen, fireman of the express, 'but it was too late.' He and the driver jammed the brakes hard over and, at the last second, jumped for their lives. The trains collided at around 30 mph, and the results were horrendous. The engine of the express reared up and mounted the second carriage of the other train, and such was the impact that the boilers of both locomotives were torn away. The first four coaches of the express were telescoped, and a coach from the local train was hurled off the rails on to the bank. 'There was a terrible crash and I found myself dazed and bruised and lying in a field,' said a railway official on the express. 'When I looked around my blood ran cold. The shrieks and cries of the dying were heart-rending. They were worse than anything I ever heard in France.'

The guns had been silent only just over two years, and comparisons with the battlefield came readily to mind. 'We saw some awful sights in the war, and this was like the ghastliness of it all over again,' said one of six disabled soldiers who had been travelling to Newtown for orthopaedic treatment and escaped unhurt from the wreck. A blinded soldier said simply: 'I thanked God for once I couldn't see.'

A clergyman with an axe rescued many people from the wreckage, and the small minority of people who owned cars in the neighbourhood drove to the scene and took the injured to hospital. The passengers fortunate enough to escape injury tore at the twisted metal and splintered woodwork to rescue the victims. 'Among those we succeeded in releasing was a boy of about seven, who was too dazed to utter a word,' said R. D. Williams, of Aberystwyth. A youth of 17 trapped in the wreckage for hours while rescuers struggled to free him was brought out alive, only to die in hospital next day. 'The train looks for all the world as though it had been shelled by heavy guns and suffered direct hits,' wrote a reporter.

In theory, the accident was impossible. The Cambrian Railways had conformed perfectly with the safety principles of the time by installing Tyer's electric train tablet instruments, No 6 pattern, on the predominantly single track from Whitchurch to the coast. These ensured that no more than one train could be on a stretch of single track at any given time, if the system was worked correctly. The instruments at each end of a section were electrically connected so that only one tablet could be released at a time. Thus, when a driver was given a tablet he knew the line ahead was clear. As an extra safety precaution, the instruments also had electric indicators showing the state of the line. They read 'Tablet Out' or 'Tablet In' so that the merest glance would show if a train were travelling in either direction. For over thirty years, since the passing of the Regulation of Railways Act of 1889 following the Armagh disaster, which killed 78 people, the line had been safely worked

with this system. Only those 'spirits of carelessness and irresponsibility'
brought this proud record to an end.

At the time of the accident Abermule station was staffed by a relief
stationmaster and a signalman, both experienced men, a 15-year-old
booking clerk and a 17-year-old porter. Only the stationmaster and
signalman were authorised to work the tablet system, but it was clear from
the events of the day that this rule was habitually being ignored. Just before
noon the signalman at Montgomery, east of Abermule, sought permission
for the stopping train from Whitchurch to enter the Montgomery-
Abermule section, and his opposite number at Abermule agreed. The tablet
was thus withdrawn at Montgomery and the train went on its way. The
Abermule signalman then established that the express from Aberystwyth
had left Moat Lane on its way to Newtown, four miles west of Abermule. It
was on time and there was, on the face of it, nothing to prevent the two
trains crossing safely at Abermule, as usual. The signalman told the two lads
the position of the two trains and then left the platform to go to the signal
box. The stationmaster returned from lunch but no-one told him where the
trains were. He was nowhere in the vicinity when there was a call from
Newtown asking if the express could enter the Newtown-Abermule section,
so the porter took it upon himself to give permission. He then left for the

ground frame which operated the points and signals at the west end of the station, telling no-one what he had done. The evidence of these activities, however, was there for all to see on the electric indicators, which showed 'Tablet Out' for both the Newtown-Abermule and Montgomery-Abermule sections.

When the stopping train arrived from Montgomery, the booking clerk took the tablet from the driver — another breach of regulations. On his way to the tablet room, where he meant to place it immediately in the instrument, he came across the stationmaster. The lad was keen to return to his proper task of collecting the tickets from passengers leaving the train, so he said, 'Change this tablet while I go and get the tickets.' At least, that was his story. The stationmaster insisted that the boy said, 'Take this tablet for the down train; he's going on.' This, to his mind, meant that the express had been delayed and the stopping train was going on to Newtown. The fatal error he made was in assuming that the tablet in his hand was the one for the Newtown-Abermule section; had he looked at it he would have seen that it was for the Montgomery-Abermule section. He handed it to the driver of the stopping train. Amazingly, he didn't look at it either, and neither did the fireman. By their carelessness they signed their own death warrants.

'In all my experience,' said Colonel Pringle, representing the Ministry of Transport at the inquest, 'I have never known a driver to receive and take the wrong tablet for a section.' The porter and booking clerk were found guilty of negligence and excess of duty, and the acting stationmaster and signalman came close to being arraigned for manslaughter. In the end, however, they were found guilty of 'great neglect which calls for the most severe censure,' a verdict spiritedly condemned as too lenient by the *Montgomeryshire Express*.

'The very simpleness of this calamitous failure,' said the paper in a leading article, 'introduces a new feeling of dread among the travelling public.' In time the feeling passed, but the lessons of Abermule were not forgotten.

11 Great Days of Steam

T HE GREAT WAR OF 1914-18 brought many things to an end, and a few years after the slaughter the British public found that a railway system which had been cosily familiar was gone for ever. Government control of railways during the hostilities, accepted as a patriotic necessity even by those who would have regarded any kind of state control in peace-time as the eighth deadly sin, paved the way for the Railways Act of 1921. This was 'rationalisation' on a huge scale, although the word did not then have the common currency it achieved later. Railway companies by the dozen, from the little Burry Port and Gwendraeth Valley to the mighty LNWR, became no more than names in the history book. The Cambrian, the Rhymney, the Taff Vale and the Barry — the world no longer had a use for them, for all the wealth of their traditions and the smartness of their livery.

Only the mulishly obstinate and the shamelessly romantic failed to admit that their extinction was inevitable. The railways which had played such a conspicuous part in Britain's war effort were plainly in need of the kind of money which the multiplicity of companies simply could not provide. True, they were in better shape than those in many other European countries, but this served only to emphasise the bitter toll in lives and property that the Great War had taken. So, with the minimum of fuss, Lloyd George's Coalition Government introduced the Act which put the railways in the hands of the Big Four: the Great Western, the London Midland and Scottish, the London and North Eastern and the Southern. A contemporary writer saw them as 'four great soulless combines', but on both sides of the political spectrum — if for different reasons — the logic of the groupings was accepted. On the Left, they were seen as a step on the road to state ownership; on the Right, as good business.

In Wales, travelling by rail — except on some narrow-gauge lines — now meant going by GWR or LMS. The LMS had the important Holyhead and Central Wales lines, but overall the GWR was predominant. Strictly speaking, the leading independent companies entered the Great Western kingdom as constituent rather than absorbed companies, but while this may have been a balm to wounded pride it meant little in practice. Of the 25 directors, 19 were from the GWR and one each from the six constituent companies: the Cambrian, the Taff Vale, the Barry, the Rhymney, the Alexandra (Newport and South Wales) Docks and Railways, and the Cardiff Railway — a late and not very distinguished enterprise by the Bute trustees. The B & M, for all its character, was not a constituent company, and neither was the Neath and Brecon, but so far as the traveller was concerned it made not a scrap of difference. He, or she, went by GWR, and that was the end of it.

This domination of the GWR over its minions meant that the newly-expanded company found the going much easier than the LMS, which brought together two deadly rivals of more or less equal status, the LNWR and the Midland. For those even moderately well versed in railway lore, this was an attempt to reconcile the irreconcilable. Even the name of London Midland and Scottish was not arrived at without effort. The GWR, however, seemed to exist almost by divine right, and in its strength and confidence it set about reviving the old elegance of its expresses. Chimneys were

The Fishguard Express.
(Pronto Photo History).

given polished copper tops, and brasses shone. In 1923 the Castle class locomotives appeared, and the *Caerphilly Castle* was hailed as the 'most powerful locomotive in Britain.' The name was significant, because Caerphilly had
an important place in the GWR scheme of things: its locomotive works, previously belonging to the Rhymney Railway, became a by-word for crafts-
manship.

This was a time of restless innovation when rail, in spite of increasing
competition from road transport, was still supreme. The Castles were fine
machines, but the time came when the general manager of the GWR, Sir
Felix Pole, wanted something finer still. So the Kings were born, and the
first of the four-cylinder 4-6-0 class, *King George V*, was shipped to America
from Roath Dock, Cardiff, in 1927 to take part in the centenary of the Baltimore and Ohio railroad. It awoke ardent feelings in the heart of a writer in
the *New York Herald Tribune*.

'Somewhere in the breast of every normal homo sapiens there stretches a
chord that vibrates only to the sight of a fine locomotive. Even now, with air-
planes and motors to bid against it in its own field of romantic interest, the
steam locomotive retains its fascination... Man has devised no other

machine that expresses its feelings so frankly and unmistakeably. A locomotive sighs, it pants, it coughs, it barks; it emits impassioned shrieks and mournful toots; it puts forth powerful staccato protests at hauling a heavy load or climbing a steep grade; it purrs ecstatically as it romps along the rails at a mile a minute; it can hiss and throb and snort and tinkle. And in addition to all these auditory forms of expression it has its visual signs, its plumes of steam spelling surplus energy, its belchings of black smoke denoting determination, its sparks at night registering passion.'

Eight years later the Great Western celebrated its centenary, and a book brought out by the company to mark the occasion was marvellously evocative of the times. In his foreword the GWR chairman, Sir Robert Horne, noted that in the past hundred years 'all the civilised portions of the globe have become covered by networks of railways.' With the introduction of telephones and telegraphs and fast transport by land, sea and air, it had been 'the most fruitful era in history in its application of the advances of science to the satisfaction of human needs and aspirations.' The railway was the forerunner of all this progress, and he was confident it could face the challenge of the internal combustion engine. 'If some people are now inclined to say that the days of the railway are numbered, it is only because their minds are confused by the rapid advance of these exciting times. The

Western Region's holiday special, the Pembroke Coast Express, between Newport and the Severn Tunnel.
(Photo: J. E. Martin, Cardiff).

A South Wales express headed by engine No. 5049, Denbigh Castle, entering Swansea. Early 1950s. (Photo: J. E. Martin, Cardiff).

truth is that more than ever, the railways are vital to the transport system of every country and are essential to the efficient functioning of all the newer services. Wherever passengers have to be transported in large numbers or goods conveyed in great volume, the railways provide not merely the most economical but the only practical method of carriage: and to all reflecting minds it will be apparent that the future of efficient and economical transport depends upon close co-operation between all systems of conveyance by rail, road and air. In the ultimate resort all transport is one, and, while not indivisible, can only reach perfection when its essential unity is realized.'

These prescient words came at a time when all four main line companies were complaining about unfair competition from road transport. They pointed out that hauliers paid only part of the cost of road maintenance through licence and petrol duties, whereas the railway companies had to foot the bill themselves for the upkeep of the permanent way. Moreover, railways had to pay local rates in every district through which their lines ran, whereas road hauliers escaped this particular burden. It would have been too

A Capitals United at speed, heading for Cardiff in the 1950s. (Photo: J. E. Martin, Cardiff).

much, perhaps, to expect the railway directors to appreciate a kind of poetic justice in this. A century earlier, it had been the coaching interests which had complained of unfair competition from rail companies, which were taxed much less severely than the proprietors of stage coaches.

The GWR, at least, had had the good sense to realise that motor buses were not to be wished away. It was one of the first companies to co-ordinate rail and road transport in rural areas, and even before the first world war its own lorries ran from Llandyssul to New Quay and Haverfordwest to St David's with parcels and goods. In the Twenties combined road and rail excursions became commonplace, and in 1933 the future took shape with the introduction of diesel traction between Paddington and Didcot. This experimental railcar, with a powerful four-stroke engine, was such a success that the company was encouraged to promote the first express diesel rail-cars in Britain on the Cardiff-Birmingham run in 1934. Carrying 120 passengers — mainly businessmen — in superior third-class accommodation, they stopped only at Newport and Gloucester and were capable of speeds up to 80 mph. 'This invention,' wrote Sir Robert Horne, 'makes it possible to give express services between points where the number of passengers is not large enough to require the employment of a train drawn by a powerful steam engine.' Even his imagination balked, however, at the thought of diesel expresses thundering along main lines, for he added,' . . . .

let nobody imagine that the days of the steam locomotive are done or even declining.'

These were, in fact, the great days of steam. In the summer of 1938 the quickest expresses went from London to Cardiff in only 152 minutes, compared with 160 minutes in 1927 and 170 minutes in 1914. Rail travel had reached new levels of sophistication, with dining cars seating 119 people at a time and the 'novelty' of the newly-introduced buffet cars which, claimed the GWR, were 'luxuriously fitted like some of the snack bars in the West End of London'. Passengers sat at a long counter and chose their food from dishes displayed in glass showcases. The first buffet cars ran only the shorter routes, the company evidently believing that passengers facing a journey of any length would not be content simply with a snack if they intended buying a meal at all.

Sleeping accommodation, by this time, was no longer simply the preserve of the rich. The third-class sleeping car had not made its appearance until after the First World War but now people were quite used to it. 'The men change into pyjamas without a trace of self-consciousness; they turn in as systematically as if at home,' observed one of the anonymous writers in that GWR centenary publication, entitled *Great Western Progress*. He went on:

An Up South Wales Pullman, headed by a Castle, approaching Newport in the 1950s.
(Photo: J. E. Martin, Cardiff).

The Birmingham — Cardiff rail car in 1934.
(Pronto Photo History).

'Railway journeys have long ceased to be the adventure they were in the days of footwarmers. It is odd to recall how women, who in a public conveyance are now every bit as self-possessed as men, till the beginning of the century went on railway journeys equipped as for exploration of unknown continents. They sometimes travelled with bundles of blankets and sheets, for use not in the train but at the end of the journey, so that they could be sure the bedding would be properly aired. If they were travelling alone the stowing of their luggage in the van was watched with anxious eyes, they were tucked inside rugs with a supply of foodstuffs at hand, and instructions were given to the guard about them. There are specimens still in existence of the travelling teapot, with the small hay-box that kept it warm, which sometimes accompanied the intrepid woman passenger. At a wayside station a porter would be sent for hot water, with which she made the tea . . .

'If class distinctions in travel have not wholly disappeared, the dividing lines become less rigid with the years. The second-class compartment survives chiefly on suburban lines, the first-class compartment everywhere; but their proportions are small indeed compared with the democratic third. In one month this year* the British railways carried roughly one million first-class, 113,000 second-class and 61 million third-class passengers. It is said that when men can afford to travel first they usually do so for the sake of comfort, whether alone or in company. Their womenfolk when paying for themselves travel third as a rule, especially on shopping expeditions from suburb to town.

---

* 1935.

'Fewer first-class passengers mean fewer good-sized tips for porters. On the other hand, third-class travellers give sixpences and shillings today where they once gave coppers. The younger generation are reported to tip less freely than their elders, women less so than men. Now that so much heavy luggage goes in advance and compact suitcases can be carried by their owners it is not so common as it once was to see porters staggering under mountainous burdens. In the Victorian era *Punch* would scarcely have been recognizable without its pictures and jokes about these much-tried men.'

One result of the groupings brought about by the Railways Act of 1921 was the increase in through services. Before the First World War, a long journey could mean frequent changes of train and interminable periods of waiting at draughty junctions. By 1935, however, the GWR was able to boast that there were through coaches or through trains to all parts of its vast system. There were nearly 60 points of exchange with the LMS, 15 with the Southern and seven with the LNER. There were through expresses from Newcastle to Cardiff and Swansea thanks to co-operation with the LNER, an important business link between the South Wales ports and those of the north-east coast.

Track maintenance required constant industry and vigilance. At that time, every year over 400 miles of track were being relaid on the GWR alone. Eighty of its 10,500 bridges were reconstructed annually and tunnel maintenance was a high priority. For the first three months of the year, the engineers had complete possession of the Severn Tunnel every Sunday to enable them to carry out track renewals and other repairs. Even the most patient of travellers was hard put not to grumble as the re-routed train made its long, tedious detour through Chepstow and Gloucester.

The days of steam can be seen through many eyes, but the men who actually worked the trains tend to be overlooked. When Sir Robert Horne was dictating his foreword to that GWR history in his comfortable office, for example, Edmund Lewis was driving trains between Brecon and Cardiff. He had started his working life on the old Brecon and Merthyr Railway as a cleaner in 1908 — '12 bob a week for 12 hours a day, and you had to make it 12 hours before you had the money,' he recalled in the summer of 1979, when he was in his 87th year.

'They were good engines on the B & M only some of them were in a rough state, especially when the war came on — they were working night and day and not much repairs done to them and so on. Working on heavy loads too at Talybont bank. There was no messing about there. Seven miles of it, one in 38 all the way.'

Was it a difficult line to work?

'Well, you wanted to know where you were working. A goods train could get away with you and you'd never stop them after. The gradient was ups and downs sort of thing, see — passenger train wasn't so bad with the vacuum

The King George V.
(Pronto Photo History).

(brake) like but on the ordinary goods train if you had a train of coal or something heavy and you give 'em a run you'd never hold 'em. The train was
braked by the guard at the top of the bank see to go down the bank. You were
allowed 50 minutes up the bank and 50 minutes down, but they wouldn't
grumble if you took over the time so long as you said you had bad brakes or
something like that.'

Was he glad or sorry when the B & M was taken over by the GWR?

'Well I don't know about glad or sorry . . . It was all right on the B & M but
the Great Western was a fine company to work for and they had better stuff
too — better engines and all that. When you had an engine coming here
from Swindon it was more like a clock or watch than an engine — boss of the
job and do any work.

'This last lot of engines they built when Sir Felix Pole was the general

manager — the 56 class engine — they were built for the South Wales coal traffic. They were strong engines and good engines . . .'

Did any passengers want to travel with him on the footplate?

"Oh some did! We weren't suppose to have 'em but we did. On the QT! I can remember doing one job in a snowstorm — I'm not supposed to tell you this but I'm telling you — they couldn't say much about it today anyway . . . Well, the lines were all blocked round here — this was in 1947 — and they sent me down on the Rhymney section to Quakers Yard. We went through a lot of drifts up to the footplate, and when I got to Quakers Yard the foreman come up to me and said, 'Hey, do us a favour, can you?' I said, 'What's that?' He said 'I've got ten colliers in here from Trelewis colliery and they want to get back to Merthyr. Can you take 'em?' I said 'Aye, try to . . .' So I said to my mate, 'Harry, shove the box of coal into the firebox — we won't be able to fire after these fellers come on . . .' Then the foreman said, 'Hey, I'm coming another favour — I've got a nurse from Merthyr Hospital, will you take her as well?' I said 'Oh crikey — right-o,' so I took the lot on.

'Anyway, when I stopped outside here by Rhydycar I could see the signal was up. Lewis the ganger come up on the engine to me and he said, 'Eddie, you're not in a hurry, are you? There's a passenger train with colliers coming in." So I said, "Get up on the step by here, Lewis, and take a look at this lot" — there they were, a nurse and ten colliers all on one engine.'

Mr Lewis was talking in the kitchen of his home in Heolgerrig, Merthyr Tydfil, where he liked to sit close to the fire. He recalled some of the more unusual tricks of the trade.

'When we booked on at four o'clock in the morning we'd do the shunting and get to Torpantau and generally stop on top of the bank for the passenger to come up. So we'd have our bit of breakfast there — fry-up. I'd have half a dozen kippers there on the shovel — three or four for my mate, three or four for me. Fry 'em on the engine shovel in the firebox and sit down and eat 'em there — get a lump of fat with 'em and make a good breakfast — you'd think you were in the Savoy Hotel. I was one of the leading lights on that lark, frying up the kippers. I'd take a bit of bacon sometimes or an egg as well, but it was the kippers I enjoyed. Oh, there was lots of tricks done there they didn't know nothing about!'

When Edmund Lewis was chugging up and down the Valleys, David

The South Wales Red Dragon.
(Pronto Photo History).

Western Standard Pacific, (4-6-2), No. 70027, Rising Star, at the head of a Red Dragon express.
(Photo: J. E. Martin, Cardiff).

Owen — two years his junior — was driving for the LMS on the Central Wales line. At 85, he too had a keen brain and a host of vivid memories. At his home in Carmarthen, he recalled how he had started work there in 1910 as a cleaner in the locomotive department of the LNWR. Two or three years later, he became a fireman at three shillings a day for a 60 hour week.

'We'd burn about five tons of coal a night. That was a proposition. It wasn't just shovelling it — you had to direct it to the proper corners, you know,. And of course all the engines, the steam engines — they had what we fellows called a soul.' He chuckled. 'Aye . . . and every one different, you see. One would be a very good runner. Another of the same class would have qualities for picking up the train rapidly. And others were very good riders. We knew all the peculiarities and kept them in our minds and some of the older drivers used to keep a little notebook where they put down, say, number 1754 bad for steaming — so that they had their characters written out for them, you see, written out for them — yes . . .'

In those days, he said, Carmarthen was an important junction. 'I can remember the station being filled and the roadways leading up to it on three occasions. One was when a Catholic cardinal was on his way to Ireland in the night train. All the Catholics were congregated and he came out to bless them. Another was when the First World War broke out and the Belgian

Welsh excursion train at Old Oak in 1925.
(Pronto Photo History).

refugees came here. The first one that stepped on the platform was a man with a heavy drooping moustache named Mr Schoolmaster, and his family still remains in the district. The third occasion was when the first wounded came back from the First World War, and the roadways were filled with people right up there. Of course, the railways made for a social centre in those days and when anything happened invariably the local railway would be associated with it.'

The climb up to the Sugar Loaf tunnel on the Central Wales was something never to be forgotten. 'It was very hard work,' said another veteran, Mozart Thomas, of Llandovery, who had just started work as an engine cleaner when the First World War came to an end. 'And if it was a warm day going through the tunnel it was enough to smother you with the fumes and you were glad to get out. Even on a cold winter's night you'd be perspiring in the tunnel and sometimes you had to put your coat over your head because it was that hot. They say the roof of the Sugar Loaf was too low, you know, too low on to the chimney stack. I've known firemen faint because of the hard work, and they would lie down on the floor a bit and then come to.'

Had he ever known a driver faint?

'No, I don't think I ever heard of a driver faint because he was in a corner there and the majority of them you see had a handkerchief over their nose — they'd just hold a handkerchief over it.'

Did he dread the Sugar Loaf tunnel?

'Oh yes. It was hard graft and the perspiration was dripping off you and you were soaking wet and especially when you were on the bank engine in the rear . . . you had to come down and face the wind, you know, no shelter at all. It's a wonder to me that we all never caught pneumonia.'

Sometimes trains would break down in the tunnel. 'Nothing could happen if you carried out the rules but if you didn't you were in trouble. You had to contact the guard on a gradient like that for him to put sufficient brakes on so that the rear end wouldn't run back. You uncoupled a couple of wagons and took what you could to Llanwrtyd and then fetched the rest.'

He talked about the difficulty of working a steep gradient. 'The skill was not to break loose and break the couplings. You had to watch the weight of the train. If you come over the hump a bit too fast coming down it snapped the couplings quite easily.'

Had he known any runaway trains on the Sugar Loaf line? 'Yes, a pig iron train. They didn't put sufficient brakes on the wagon at Sugar Loaf to come down, so the driver had no control. They went through the block at Cynghordy half-way down and there was an engine and about ten wagons in the field and the rest blocking the road. Nobody was hurt — the driver and fireman jumped, and the guard jumped.'

And the characters he'd known on the railway? 'Oh crikey, I could be stuck all day telling you. In those days you had to be a good fireman or some of the drivers wouldn't take you. They wouldn't bend down and fire the engine themselves, you know — they'd just go to the foreman and say, 'I'm not taking that chap, he's not capable enough.' And some drivers would slip off for a pint and leave you in charge in certain stations.

'Characters . . . well, there was old Poopsie. Tom Jones Poopsie. He was always jovial and he'd do anything for you. He used to drink in the old White Lion and he had a dog and when she had pups he used to say, 'Come and see my poopsies' and they called him that then. And there was old Ianto Prytherch. He was a big strong man and if there was a fair about anywhere with a boxing booth he'd go in and he'd hammer all of them — hammer them all old Ianto Prytherch would.'

In the Second World War there were heavy loads on the line. 'Oh terrible, yes. Up and down. If there was an ammunition train coming through the tunnel you used to have three engines for brake power because they dare not couple the brakes up on the wagons in case the sparks would ignite the ammunition in the vans.'

Were the trains ever attacked by enemy aircraft? 'Well, my only recollection of a bombing was an ammunition train one Sunday night standing at the down home signal of the south box in Llandovery. The Jerry dropped five bombs right around, one about a hundred yards from the engine. But I was coming down on an ammunition train one night and we were crossing the viaduct when old Jerry dropped a flare. Good job it was a misty night — he never seen us — and the driver of one of the engines never come over the road again, he was so frightened when he seen the flare — well, you could see the little chapel underneath the viaduct — you could see it like daylight. And

*Autorail ('Push-and-Pull')
unit at Fishguard Station, en
route for Clarbeston Road,
junction for the Milford
Haven — Paddington line.
About 1943. Locomotive No.
1452 (0-4-2 T Class).*
(Photo: J. E. Martin, Cardiff)

the Home Guard there who was seeing nobody blew up the tunnel run for his life.

'Mostly these ammunition trains were coming along from the north of Scotland to Swansea docks for the stuff to be shipped abroad.'

He too had vivid memories of the hard winter of 1947. 'We were going up the line and it was raining and freezing the same time and your coat froze on your back and the little birds were frozen to the tree branches.'

It was a hard life then on the old Sugar Loaf line? 'Oh, you earned your money, you know. I look back and I often say I'd never do it again. What killed us mostly was during the war we had such poor coal we had to clean the fire frequently to get steam — the old coal used to clinker up quickly and there was no heat in it and then you had to clean the clinkers out and it was a terrible job, one mass of perspiration. Broke your heart very near that did, broke your heart.'

When Ellis Powell joined the GWR just before the outbreak of the Second World War, he was following a family tradition. 'My father was a plate-layer,' he said at his home in Heol Rudd, Carmarthen. 'It was quite an achievement to get a job on the railways when I was a boy because it was a job for life.

'We were proud to belong to the Great Western. We were regarded as the elite of the railway companies of the time. We had a better pension scheme and a stricter medical examination. Standards demanded of us were higher, I believe, and we were able to retire at 60, not 65 as it is now, of course. So our position has rather worsened under the new set-up.'

He started as an engine cleaner — 'a dirty job at times but nevertheless it was part and parcel of the line of promotion; from engine cleaner to fireman, from fireman to passenger fireman and from passenger fireman to driver.

'Firing was a very skilled job indeed. It wasn't just a question of shoving coal in willy-nilly, and the old drivers who taught us our job would see to it that you did your job properly.

'Preparation of your locomotive was the main part, I suppose. You booked on for your shift and you had a certain head of steam in your locomotive but you had to build it up gradually. The fire would have to be spread right over the firebox to build it up with lumps of coal the right size and the right amount. It was no good throwing in lumps of coal any size and as many as you wished — you had to build up your fire properly in order that you had a full head of steam when it was required. The biggest disgrace to any foot-plateman was to be known to have come to a standstill through insufficient steam. This was something we all avoided like the plague.'

War-time meant arduous working conditions. 'The black-out was pretty grim all round but more so to us, I suppose, because we had to make sure no fire or light was to be seen. We were provided with a tarpaulin which had to be positioned before each trip. It went from the cab roof to the tender and along the sides of the cab as well, and not only was that an inconvenience but the heat at times through lack of air meant that you were working under very hot conditions indeed.

'The other factor was that the quality of the coal was so inferior. We used to get the best quality steam coal before the war. Now in war-time because of the needs of industry, the war effort and so on we had to contend with the fifth grade of coal. The performance of the engine was retarded, there was a quicker clinkering up of the fire and all in all it meant that each one had to make the best he could with inferior tools and inferior equipment.'

The engines, as well as the men, had to be tough to stand up to the strain. 'We were working at maximum capacity. We hadn't done that before, we haven't done it since. Trains were fully loaded, both passenger and freight. In those days the mail at night would be eleven to thirteen coaches.'

And the goods trains? 'Oh, 70 coal wagons was the order of the day. We could relate many stories of trains limping home on a wing and a prayer. I can remember crawling into Carmarthen Junction myself with a goods train when we had more wagons in number than pounds of steam on the clock.'

It was a milestone in his life when he was promoted from fireman to driver in 1955. 'It was the same for us all. You'd achieved something you'd aspired to from the very beginning.'

Did he take a pride in the engines? 'Oh yes, yes, because each engine performed differently. You had to exercise a measure of skill. Some engines had to be encouraged to give the best possible performance. No two engines reacted in exactly the same way although they were of the same type. And no engine would act identically from day to day. They were most temperamental and they had to be encouraged and cultivated and nursed.'

For many years he worked the branch line from Carmarthen to Aberystwyth. 'A lovely line to work over. It had its difficulties, mind. It had very severe curves and could be a rough ride on times but the scenery compensated for any discomfort.'

Did he make friends with the regular passengers? 'Yes indeed, and some of the boys met their wives in this way. You must remember that the young fireman was quite a hero in his day!'

He talked of the bond that developed between driver and fireman, who could work together as a team for years on end. 'They endured some difficult times together and had to show a great deal of self-reliance, as there was never a boss around to tell them what to do. And here's an interesting thing. Before the Second World War, no father and son would be allowed to work together.'

Ellis Powell drove many classes of locomotive. 'I think the Hall class was my favourite because it was a general purpose engine. It could work freight and passengers — a very successful type of engine introduced by the Great Western.'

How did he rate the Castle? 'Quite a good engine to drive. It had something the other engines didn't have — it had a speedometer, and wipers to the windows. But if you were to ask me about the firing of the Castle class engine — now here was really a hard job of work. They were heavy in consumption of coal and to keep a full head of steam for a full shift with a Castle demanded the very best and a lot of exertion on the part of the fireman. Mind, the Castle class engine looked very regal and majestic, didn't it? It was the showpiece!'

12 Rail Revivals

T HE CASTLES, FOR ALL THEIR SPLENDOUR, could not last for
ever. The steam power they symbolised was fated to pass, though not
without heartache and misgivings on the part of experienced railwaymen. Yet while it disappeared from the main lines, it survived in out-of-the-
way places thanks to the energy and imagination of zealots who won themselves the title of 'railway preservationists'. At first there were just a few of
them, inspired by blind faith and spurred on by that devotion which those
who regard railways as just another form of transport find inexplicable.
Later there were many, and the lines they saved grew in stature from screw-
ball enterprises to businesses with a recognised role in the Welsh economy.
They became the Great Little Trains of Wales, publicised for their contribution to the development of tourism in the Principality.

The movement began in Talyllyn, where the little railway which had been
in existence nearly a century had managed to survive only because its owner,
Sir Haydn Jones, was prepared to lose money on it. During the Second
World War there were two trains a day on Mondays, Wednesdays and
Fridays in summer and a slender winter service on two days a week. The
original Fletcher Jennings locomotives, No 1 *Talyllyn* and No 2 *Dolgoch,*
were still in business, but by 1945 they were badly in need of overhaul and Sir
Haydn wasn't prepared to spend money on both. His choice fell on *Dolgoch,*
which was sent to the Atlas Foundry at Shrewsbury. When the Transport
Bill for nationalising the railways was published the engineer and author L.
T. C. Rolt, whose interests took in vintage cars and canals as well as railways,
noticed that by some bureaucratic oversight the Talyllyn was not included. A
sturdy opponent of state ownership, which he saw as another step in the
grey standardisation of British life, he pointed out this omission to two
friends, Bill Trinder and Jim Russell. Rolt made a number of visits to Towyn,
and in his book *Railway Adventure* he described his one and only meeting
with Sir Haydn Jones, who was Liberal M.P. for Merioneth from 1910-45. It
took place in an old-fashioned office above the post office in Towyn, where

Sir Haydn, an imposing figure with snow-white hair, fly-away collar, pin-stripe trousers and black coat, told him that in spite of the losses he would continue to run a summer service as long as he lived. Since he was then in his eighties, however, this assurance clearly had its limitations. The day-to-day task of running the railway had been entrusted to Edward Thomas, a general factotum who sold the tickets, kept the accounts and was also stationmaster and guard. Rolt has a delightful description of him finishing the day's work at Towyn Wharf.

'When the last passenger had been booked in he clapped on his trilby hat, locked the office and walked briskly towards the waiting train with the cash takings in a linen bag tightly clasped by the neck. Before hopping nimbly into the brake van it was his invariable custom to signal the "right away" by a quick, peremptory flick of the wrist of his free hand, as though he were shooing the train away like some disobedient dog. This little gesture seemed to be just as effective as the more orthodox ritual of whistle and flag, for it was immediately answered by a shrill toot from *Dolgoch*. Then with a sigh of steam from cylinder cocks and leaking glands and the creak and snatch of tautening couplings, the ancient train gathered itself together and lumbered away under the bridge on yet another journey up the valley.'

In the summer of 1950 Sir Haydn died, and it was time for action. Rolt and Trinder went to Towyn, where Thomas told them that the railway was extremely unlikely to open the following year. Rolt and his friends called a public meeting in Birmingham and a committee was set up to begin negotiations with Sir Haydn's executors. Thus the Talyllyn Railway Preservation Society was born. An appeal was launched through letters to the Press, including one to *The Times* in February 1951 pointing out that the railway was now the oldest narrow-gauge passenger steam line in the world and among the very few independent companies surviving in the British Isles.

'The original locomotives and rolling stock are still in use,' Rolt's letter ran. 'Following the death last year of Sir Haydn Jones, who was general manager and sole shareholder, efforts have been made to ensure that this historic railway shall not close. To this end the Talyllyn Railway Preservation Society has been formed to raise funds and voluntary labour to repair the track and to maintain and augment the locomotives and rolling stock. Meanwhile the old railway company will continue in being on a non-profitmaking basis and will be administered jointly by representatives of the society and of the late Sir Haydn Jones. The society is relying upon wide support from the public in order to realize its ultimate aim, which is to make the Talyllyn Railway a living example of the old railway companies, as they were in the days before the amalgamations of 1921.'

The support he sought was immediately forthcoming, yet the problems were daunting. The track had to be relaid, and locomotives were a pressing

Opposite:
A combination of steam and scenic splendour on the Festiniog. The locomotive Blanche crosses the viaduct at Tanybwlch.

need. The Talyllyn was in such a bad state that it was doubtful it could ever be brought back into working order, and the *Dolgoch* could not cope alone with the ambitious service planned for the summer of 1951. History, however, provided a stroke of luck. Over the mountain were the remains of the Corris Railway, also built to the unusual 2 ft 3 in gauge. It had closed in August 1948, but the scrap merchants who had acquired the rails agreed to sell some of them to the Talyllyn society. More significantly, the two Corris 0-4-2 saddle tank engines were discovered rusting away in a yard — rather the worse for wear, but basically in sound condition. Rolt tells of their trip to Swindon, where against all probability a British Railways executive allowed the society to buy both engines for less than the price originally asked for each. They were taken to Towyn and named *Sir Haydn* and *Edward Thomas*. Fortune was now beginning to favour the brave, and it was regarded as a lucky break of the first order when the boiler of the *Dolgoch* was officially inspected and approved for service at a working pressure of 100 lb per square inch. Rolt put this down to the fact that those sturdy Cumbrian engineers, back in Victorian times, had given it a copper firebox, brass tubes and an outer box and barrel of Lowmoor iron.

On a cloudless Whit Monday in 1951 the revitalised railway was officially opened, the *Dolgoch* pulling four coaches and a brake van to Rhydyronen. Services proper began on the first Monday in June along the whole length from Towyn to Abergynolwyn. In the first year there was a record total of 15,000 passenger journeys and this increased to 22,000 the following year, with revenue in four figures. Success was achieved with a regular staff of three at the beginning of June rising to seven in the peak season, and a small band of volunteers working up to 12 hours a day for seven days a week, with scarcely a meal break. 'Our small company,' wrote Rolt in *Railway Adventure,* 'was recruited from many widely separated walks of life; undergraduates, shopkeepers, clergymen, engineers, railwaymen and schoolmasters worked side by side with us, and neither among volunteers nor staff was there any hierarchy or nice distinction.'

Some of these volunteers already had their eyes on a disused railway twenty-five miles to the north: the Festiniog, which had closed in 1946 after years of struggle. This historic railway had, it seemed, finally reached the end of the line. After the last freight train had run down to Porthmadog the rolling stock was left where it stood, at the mercy of vandals, souvenir hunters and the weather. Name plates and number plates vanished, windows were smashed, and what humanity left behind nature took over. The track was overgrown with weeds, sturdy saplings flourished, and cuttings were ablaze with rhododendrons. Yet enough remained to convince those of discerning eye that this beautifully-engineered railway still held possibilities. Allan Garraway, a railwayman on Eastern Region, climbed above Tan-y-Bwlch with a friend and was convinced that, for all the appeal

of the Talyllyn, this was the railway they *ought* to be restoring. He wasn't alone in this, and by the end of 1951 a committee had been formed. Enthusiasm abounded, but money was lacking. The old company was still in existence, saddled with financial liabilities dating back to its unhappy association with the Welsh Highland Railway between the wars, and about £3,000 was needed to buy it out. Destiny, however, appeared in the shape of Alan Pegler, a board member in British Rail's Eastern Region. In what has been seen as an act of supreme eccentricity, he decided to buy the controlling shares and run the railway with the help of a voluntarily supported society. In June 1954 control of the railway passed into his hands, and six months later the Festiniog Railway Society Ltd was registered with a capital of £49 12s 6d. Pegler put his shares into a trust, which was later superseded by the Festiniog Railway Trust, a registered charity holding a majority of all shares in the company.

L. T. C. Rolt playing the role of guard on the Talyllyn Railway.
(The Times).

TAL-Y-LLYN

RAILWAY.

TIME TABLE

FOR

FEBRUARY 19TH, 1867,

And until further Notice.

Passengers to esure being booked should be at the   e minutes before the time fixed for the departure of the Trains. The times shown on his Bill are the times at which the Trains are intended to leave and arrive at the several   tions, but the Company cannot guarantee thes times being kept under any circumstances, nor will they be responsible for delay.

PASSENGERS' LUGGAGE.—The Company are not responsible unless it is booked and paid for according to its value. Each Passenger is allowed 60lbs weight of personal Luggage free of charge, the same not being Merchandise. Any excess above this weight will be charged.

For the protection of their Luggage in the Van, Passengers are requested to have their names and destination clearly stated upon, and properly fastened to each article.

The Company will not be responsible for any articles left in any of their offices for the convenience of Owners, unless deposited in the Booking Office, and the fixed charge of 2d. per Package paid.

It is requested that all Goods and Parcels be delivered at King's Station, Towyn, (and not at Pendre Station), at least half an hour before the time fixed for starting, so that they may be Booked and Signed for.

UP TRAINS.	Saturdays only.		DOWN TRAINS.	Saturdays only.	
	a.m.	p.m.	p.m,		a.m.	p.m.	p.m
Towyn (Pendre Station).. leave	9.0	1.30	6.0	Abergynolwyn ....leave	10.0	2.30	5.0
Rhydyronen	9.10	1.40	4.10	Rhydyronen	10.30	3.0	5.30
Abergynolwyn .... arrive	9.40	2.20	4.40	Towyn................arrive	10.40	3.10	5.40

N.B.--Trains do not run on Sunday.

BY ORDER.

EDWARDS, PRINTER TOWYN

The volunteers eagerly set about the task of making good all the years of neglect. The first public appeal brought in £300, and in June 1955 Garraway gave up his job in the motive power department of Eastern Region to become manager of the Festiniog, taking a 25 per cent salary cut. The railway was officially opened the following month between Porthmadog and Boston Lodge, and by the end of the summer, 21,706 passenger journeys were recorded. The figure grew to 36,671 in 1956 and 53,557 in 1957, by which time the services had been extended to Penrhyndeudraeth. Not the least satisfaction was in the fact that most of the passenger trains in the first three years were worked by one of the original locomotives, *Prince,* built in 1863 by George England.

In his lively history of the line, *The Little Wonder,* John Winton tells how much of the voluntary effort in 1956-57 went into recovering old wagons which had been left to rot; no fewer than 50 were found when the undergrowth was cleared away at Minffordd. 'The rock-bottom essence of volunteering on the Festiniog was hard physical work; shovelling, digging, wheeling a barrow, hauling out tree-trunks, cutting down branches, pulling out nettles and brambles by hand, tipping out loads of ballast, carrying heavy rails and sleepers ... there were a great many who came a few times, and a few who came a great many times,' he writes. Volunteers were organised in regional groups which to a large extent were autonomous, pursuing individual projects and publishing their own newsletters. By the end of the 1970s the society had 6,000 members, some of them living in far-distant countries. Passenger journeys had increased from 60,128 in 1958, when the line reached only as far as Tan-y-Bwlch, to 409,693 in 1978, when it went to Tanygrisiau, 12 miles from Porthmadog and only a mile from the original terminus of Blaenau Ffestiniog. Trains then ran past the Central Electricity Board's power station at Tanygrisiau, which was the subject of a prolonged legal battle between the board and the railway company — a battle which the Festiniog, against all the odds, eventually won. A new route was struck from Dduallt around Llyn Ystradau, the biggest civil engineering project ever undertaken by a preserved railway. Over the years the company had considerably increased its locomotive stock, but romantics relished the thought that the first Fairlie engine built at Boston Lodge in 1879, *Merddin Emrys,* was still going strong.

For the railway buff the terrain through which such a line passes is of secondary importance, but for tourists as a whole its appeal lies as much in the beauty of the countryside as the narrowness of the gauge and technical minutae of the locomotive. Much energy might be uselessly expended in arguing the merits of this line against that; the only valid conclusion is that the traveller is fortunate that the narrow-gauge lines thread their way through such a variety of scenery. From the day of its opening in 1902, the Vale of Rheidol Railway between Aberystwyth and Devil's Bridge was valued for its tourist potential as much as its mineral traffic. The line climbs through a wooded gorge that remains indelibly in the memory, and the sharp bends in the final stages of the journey give one the impression that at any moment the driver is about to shake hands with the guard!

In 1913 the railway was taken over by the Cambrian and after the vicissitudes of war, which made the service so unreliable that for months at a time there were no trains at all, 'Lein Fach' — as it's locally known — was absorbed by the GWR. One of the engines was scrapped, but another was restored and two more built to original designs. The harbour spur was abandoned, though one trip a year was made until 1930 to preserve the right of way. From 1931 no passenger trains ran in winter, but the summer service was so promising that in 1938 the GWR replaced the old carriages with new ones giving more spacious views of the scenery. The outbreak of war brought all services to an end, but the track and rolling stock were maintained so well that only eleven weeks after VE Day in 1945 the line was able to reopen on July 23. Trains were, however, few and far between at first, and the railway's future was in question when, in 1954, a publicity drive was launched to bring in more revenue. It was rewarded with a record number of passengers the following year, but within a decade crisis point was reached again. In December 1962 British Rail Western Region bluntly told Aberystwyth Borough Council that Lein Fach had become too heavy a burden. The council was given first option of purchase, either for itself or for a third party. The offer was kept open for three months, and in the meantime responsibility for the line passed to the London Midland Region. It was decided to maintain summer services in 1963, but in April of that year the region's district superintendent at Shrewsbury told council representatives that 5,000 extra passengers must be found. A progress committee was set up in the town, publicity in newspapers and on radio and television followed, and even before August was out the target had been exceeded. Altogether 34,237 passengers were carried in 1963, an increase of 7,388 over the previous year. Local interests survived another shock in 1967, when British Rail said they were again thinking of selling the line but changed their minds after Barbara Castle, then Minister of Transport, had seen it for herself, her visit to Aberystwyth quite fortuitously coinciding with negotiations about which she said she knew nothing. The management now said categorically that the line was not for sale, and had the satisfaction of recording 48,532 passengers and 87,703 passenger journeys the following year (a return trip, in railway parlance, counting as two passenger journeys). In 1970 the number of passenger journeys exceeded 100,000 for the first time, and climbed spectacularly to reach 179,527 in 1975. The line had the kudos of being British Rail's last remaining steam railway, with three 2-6-2 tank engines sturdily named *Owain Glyndŵr, Llywelyn* and *Prince of Wales*.

By this time the narrow-gauge revival in Wales had become a recognised success story. Its appeal lay in the fact that it showed the strength of individual effort in an age of bureaucracy and uniformity. The Welshpool and Llanfair was in business again, with two of the original engines, *The Earl* and *The Countess*, taking passengers along the five and a half miles of track which were reopened after the formation of the preservation company in 1960. There were fears that the railway's remoteness from the major tourist areas would be a handicap, but experience proved otherwise. One of the initial problems was the absence of rolling stock, for the original passenger coaches were scrapped by the GWR in 1936. The purchase of five carriages from the Admiralty's Chattenden and Upnor Railway enabled the line to reopen in 1963, and five years later a Continental touch was acquired with a set of four Austrian coaches donated by the Zillertalbahn, a railway with a fellow feeling for this little line on the Welsh border.

The next stage in the revival was marked by the reopening of part of the old Padarn Railway as the Llanberis Lake Railway in 1971. The Padarn originated in 1824 as a tramway taking slate from the Dinorwic Quarries at Llanberis to Port Dinorwic on the Menai Strait, and two 0-4-0 tender locomotives were supplied for its unusual 4 ft gauge in 1848 by Messrs Horlock. One of them, *Fire Queen,* remarkable for its absence of frames (wheels and other fittings being attached to the boiler by riveted brackets) survived the

Still going strong — the Snowdon Mountain Railway.

Another trainload of tourists makes for Devil's Bridge on the Vale of Rheidol line.

years to become a prized exhibit at the railway museum in Penrhyn Castle, near Bangor. The railway continued to operate workmen's trains until 1947 and slate trains until 1961, when three Hunslet engines acquired late in the 19th century were scrapped along with practically all the rolling stock and the entire track. The quarries at Llanberis continued to use their 1 ft 10 ¾ in system after the closure of the Padarn, but in 1967 the last three active steam engines were taken out of use and most of the company's remaining locomotives were sold for preservation. When the company went into liquidation two years later the Padarn seemed to have reached the end of the line, but a remarkable rejuvenation was to follow. The idea of a 1 ft 11 ½ in gauge railway along the track bed of the Padarn on the eastern shore of the lake received enthusiastic support, and much of the capital for the new company was raised locally. The line was re-opened in 1971, when 60,672 passenger journeys were recorded. The figure leapt to 163,948 the following year, and by the close of the decade large sums were being spent on improved facilities for visitors in association with the Padarn Country Park, in which the railway lies. Proudly heading the list of locomotives belonging to the Llanberis Lake Railway (Rheilffordd Llyn Padarn) were the three 0-4-0 Hunslet saddle tanks built between 1889 and 1922, *Elidir* — formerly *Red Damsel* — *Wild Aster* and *Dolbadarn*.

The reappearance of trains at Llyn Padarn encouraged another group of preservationists at Llyn Tegid (Bala Lake). The former Great Western line between Ruabon and Barmouth which skirted the lake had closed in 1965 following the Beeching Report, and by 1971 the track had been removed and all that remained was the ballast. An engineer working at the local creamery, however, was fired by the same kind of vision that had inspired railway revivals elsewhere. He was George Barnes, a Lancastrian by birth, who saw the tourist potential in laying a narrow gauge track where the standard gauge had been before. It so happened that the chairman of Merioneth County Council's finance committee at the time was Tom Jones, whose father had been a GWR inspector, and after a public meeting in Bala a steering committee was formed with the support of the county council. As a result Rheilffordd Llyn Tegid Cyf (Bala Lake Railway Ltd) came into being, which made history as the first company to be registered entirely in the Welsh language. When the track was put down this too was a landmark: it was the first narrow gauge track to be laid on the trackbed of a former standard gauge British Rail line. The first trains ran in 1972, with a small Ruston diesel engine donated by Glyn Williams of Blaenau Ffestiniog drawing two open sided bogie coaches. There were 4,300 passengers in the first year and 23,000 in 1973, by which time a new locomotive was in service — the *Meirionydd*, a diesel with hydraulic drive built by Severn Lamb. The appeal of steam, however, was again evident when the company bought the ex-Dinorwic Hunslet 0-4-0 *Maid Marian* from the Llanberis Lake Railway in 1975: passenger traffic increased immediately. That winter the line was extended the full length of the lake, and on August Bank Holiday Sunday in 1976 *Maid Marian* brought a five-coach train with 250 passengers aboard from Bala to Llanuwchllyn without a stop, breasting the one in 70 bank with ease. Not bad for a little engine designed in 1870 for shunting slate wagons in a quarry!

Before the 1970s were out another Welsh railway revival had taken place, unusual in that this time it was in South Wales and involved not narrow gauge but standard gauge. The Gwili Railway (Rheilffordd Gwili) was opened in 1978 along a mile of track of the old Carmarthen-Aberystwyth line between Bronwydd Arms and Cwmdwyfran. Some of those involved had belonged to the Teify Valley Preservation Society, which had hoped to

The Llanfair and Welshpool — a narrow-gauge revival in border country.
(Wales Tourist Board).

restore services between Carmarthen and Lampeter with the help of local authorities after the milk traffic had been withdrawn by British Rail early in the 1970s — passenger trains having ceased in 1965. When this scheme failed, those who refused to be daunted conceived the idea of a line from Carmarthen to Llanpumsaint and the name of Gwili Railway was adopted. The section of line they proposed to operate had originally opened in 1860 as part of the broad-gauge Carmarthen and Cardigan Railway, and had the distinction of carrying the last broad gauge trains in Wales before its conversion to standard gauge in 1872. The venture came just in time, as British Rail was about to lift the track. The first trains ran at Easter 1978 and that year 11,000 passengers were carried, although there were services only at bank holidays and summer weekends. The engine, a four coupled saddle tank by Peckett and Sons fitted with vacuum brake for passenger working, was named *Myrddin / Merlin,* the Welsh and English names being on alternate sides. A gradual extension of the line was envisaged, the long-term objective being the restoration of the track throughout from Llanpumsaint to Abergwili and, if possible, Carmarthen.

Meanwhile, the Snowdon Mountain Railway and the Fairbourne Railway continued to pull in the passengers. For the railway enthusiast, the loco-motives of the Snowdon Railway have a perennial fascination. Their idio-syncratic appearance has given rise to some lively descriptions, one admirer seeing them as 'squat little puppets that stride along, swinging their arms'. They are of two different designs, but all are standard rack tank locomotives built at Winterthur by the Swiss Locomotive and Machine Works for service on mountain railways. The oldest — *Enid, Wyddfa, Snowdon,* and *Moel Siabod* — date from the 1890s, but have stood up well to the test of time. There are nine coaches, made either in Switzerland or to Swiss design. Six were originally open above the waist, but now there are plate glass windows to protect passengers from the less balmy mountain breezes. For safety reasons, incidentally, the carriage is never coupled to the engine, which pushes it up and acts as a brake going down. Nervous passengers can rest assured, however, that each carriage is equipped with its own braking system.

The least of the Welsh railways, in size — though not in popularity, is the Fairbourne, with its diminutive 15-inch gauge. This two-mile trip beside the sea has delighted generations of holidaymakers, and the consistency of its appeal is evident in its passenger statistics. Between 1969 and 1978 an average 95,025 people travelled on the line annually, the best year being 1973 with its grand total of 112,180. The oldest engine, the 4-4-2 *Count Louis* was built in 1924 by Bassett-Lowke in Northampton. The 4-6-2 *Ernest W. Twining,* built by G & S of Stourbridge, had a career at Dudley Zoo before taking the sea breezes. The *Katie* and *Siân,* both 2-4-2 engines from G & S, bring an endearingly feminine touch to a railway which, in its capacity to sur-prise, sums up the appeal of the 'Great Little Trains'.

The Fairbourne, a toy railway, with a gauge of only 15 inches.
(Wales Tourist Board).

13 Diesel Revolution

THE RAILWAYS CAME OUT OF THE Second World War with high credit. Prime Minister Winston Churchill extolled the 'grim determination, unwavering courage, and constant resourcefulness of railwaymen of all ranks.' In spite of constant air raids, the traffic had been kept moving. The nation was thankful.

This moral capital, however, was not matched by commercial viability. Even in the uneasy peace of the Thirties, vital renewal had suffered through lack of funds for investment and the war had made the problem immeasurably worse. Apart from the losses due to war damage — estimated at over £30 million — maintenance had been neglected and the rolling stock virtually driven into the ground. Moreover, materials were scarce, skilled labour was short, and the railways were saddled with a price structure frozen at 1941 levels.

It was against this background that the Labour Government under Clement Attlee took its historic decision to nationalise the railways, along with docks, inland waterways and road haulage, in the hope of creating an 'efficient, adequate. economical and properly integrated system of public inland transport.' Instead of the Big Four railway companies, there was to be the British Transport Commission — 'a handful of men', scoffed the staunchly Tory *Western Mail,* 'who will administer the unified system henceforth to be known under the title of "British Railways".' Its leading article pursued the Right wing theme that state ownership amounted to confiscation. 'This vast property has hitherto belonged to more than one million stockholders distributed among all classes, including trustees of funds derived from the Churches, benevolent societies, pensioners, and the trade unions, who are now to receive for their holdings amounting in the aggregate to more than £1,000 million, Government compensation of a much lower nominal value, involving a serious loss of income to tens of thousands. As only about half the measure was discussed in its wild stampede through Parliament the full effects of the impact cannot be envisaged.'

Even if the railways had not been nationalised, however, the state would inevitably have been involved in their operations as the days of self-financing companies were over. Large injections of public capital would have been needed and the principle of state intervention had already been conceded with the infusion of taxpayers' money in the 1930s to help the railways modernise. In the Second World War, as in the First, the railways had been under Government control, their management being entrusted to the Railway Executive Committee. Now this gave way to the Railway Executive of the British Transport Commission, which included a trade union leader and a general as well as managers of the old companies. The new authority took command on January 1st 1948, and in the following year brought out a public relations pamphlet which defined its task as 'not revolution, but evolution.' There were 635,000 employees on the railways and over 20,000 locomotives, the vast majority of which were powered by steam. 'Diesel and diesel-electric locomotives are particularly suitable for continuous shunting duties and 65 such units are owned by British Railways . . . Britain is traditionally regarded as a "steam" country,' declared the authors, innocent of the gift of prophecy which would have enabled them to see the revolution in motive power which lay just round the corner.

In Wales, the responsibilities were shared by the London Midland Region in the north and the Western Region in the south. Broadly speaking, the former inherited the old LMS lines and the latter the GWR, but there were exceptions: the Central Wales line from Swansea and Llanelli to Shrewsbury which used to be owned by the LMS came within the province of Western Region. The passing of the Great Western was mourned by many, for it had imbued not only the general public but its own employees with a sense of something special. 'We were proud to belong to the Great Western,' an old driver recalled. 'We were regarded as the elite of all the railway companies of the time. Standards demanded of us were higher, I believe, and we were able to retire at 60, not 65. So our position worsened under the new set-up.' Some regional identity was preserved with the use of different standard colours: Western Region chocolate contrasted with London Midland maroon, North Eastern orange and Southern green.

For all the fundamental changes, much remained the same. A ride on a railway train in Britain still meant the hiss of a locomotive billowing clouds of steam at a station, the hasty shutting of windows to repel the acrid invasion of smuts and smoke in a tunnel. Brunel could have returned and felt at home, although, no doubt, he would still have mourned the death of the broad gauge. True, there were electric trains in the Southern Region and on the London Underground, but they had been around long enough to become part of the British tradition. Diesel was different. It smacked of the foreign. It was good enough for Continentals and Americans, no doubt, but the old-fashioned solidity and reliability of the steam engine seemed to suit the

British character better. Was this not, after all, the birthplace of steam locomotion? Stephenson's *Rocket* was part of the nation's folklore. Children learned at school how the young James Watt had watched the steam move a saucepan lid on his mother's kitchen range and wondered what might be achieved if this power were properly harnessed by man.

Britain, in the words of the Railway Executive, was a steam country. The Castles and Manors still thundered along the tracks, and boys playing trains waggled their arms like pistons and shrilly toot-tooted in imitation of the engine's whistle as their fathers had before them. The idea that British steam would go on for ever was given official authority by the decision to introduce a range of new standard steam classes. This huge building programme began in 1951, and anyone suggesting that these shiny new engines rolling out of the workshops were all destined for the scrapheap in the Sixties would have been thought mad.

The sense of railway tradition, reassuring in a shifting and perilous world, was confirmed by the reappearance of titled trains in the Fifties. The name of Cambrian Coast Express was restored to the Paddington-Aberystwyth run in 1951, and in the south came the Red Dragon, Capitals United and Pembroke Coast Express. Later the Pullmans made their appearance, while in the north the night Irish Mail was arriving in Holyhead at 2.25 a.m. in the winter of 1952-53, five hours and 40 minutes after steaming out of Euston. Railwaymen with long memories recalled the affectionate names given to some GWR freight trains in the Twenties: The Spud, the Ironmonger, the Ponty, the Bacon, the Up Welshman . . .

A cracking pace was achieved by the Pembroke Coast Express in 1954 — London to Newport in 128 minutes and Swansea in three hours and three-quarters. In mid Wales, the Cambrian Coast Express was reaching Aberystwyth in just under six hours from Paddington, along the line that David Davies had pioneered. And in the summer of 1955, the first Pullmans appeared in South Wales. Unlike the pre-war Great Western Pullmans in the West Country, these were designed not for holidaymakers but for businessmen. They consisted of eight coaches in chocolate and cream livery, hauled by a Castle class 4-6-0. In the early days of the service, the Pullman left Paddington at 9.55 a.m., ran non-stop to Newport and reached Swansea at 2 p.m. after halts at Cardiff and Port Talbot.

Meanwhile the Conservatives had returned to power, and competition rather than integration of transport became the objective. The Transport Act of 1953 paved the way for the return of road haulage to private ownership, and the railways were given greater freedom in fixing charges. Their finances, however, became something of a national joke. The operating return of £38 million in 1952 fell to £1.8 million in 1955, and seven years later the railways were in the red by over £100 million. By that time the change to diesel was well under way. It had been heralded by the

Modernisation Plan of 1955, which categorically stated that within a few years the building of all new steam locomotives would cease. 'The steam locomotive has in the past served the railways well,' said the BTC report. 'It has the virtues of low first cost, simplicity, robustness and long life. On the other hand, many factors combine to indicate that the end of the steam era is at hand. These include the growing shortage of large coal suitable for loco-motives; the insistent demand for a reduction in air pollution by loco-motives and for greater cleanliness in trains and railway stations; and the need for better acceleration. It is also a characteristic of steam operation that it involves hard manual labour for such tasks as the firing, cleaning and servicing of locomotives. Not only is much of this work unattractive by modern-day standards, in comparison with that offered by other industries, but it also represents an inherently wasteful use of labour resources.' Thus did the railway chiefs justify the most radical technical change in the system since the historic decision to scrap broad gauge the previous century.

To show the breadth of their vision, perhaps, there was even a reference to atomic energy in the Modernisation Plan. The authors concluded, however, that atomic powered locomotives were unlikely — to the great relief of the traditionalists, for whom the switch to diesel was quite enough. The end of steam was to be accompanied by other changes. Track and signalling were to be improved with extended use of colour-light signalling, track circuits and automatic train control, and freight services were to be drastically remodelled.

For the railwaymen, the coming of the diesel units meant going back to

Inter-City 125 leaving the Severn Tunnel in great haste. (British Railways).

school, and many of the older ones resented it. 'We had to go to Cardiff and Didcot,' said a retired driver who began work on the railways in 1917. 'There was the machine on the floor in all parts like an aeroplane engine. Oh by God, I said, how the hell am I going to get this down me?'

'People of my age adapted very quickly but the older men found it very difficult,' said a younger man. 'Several men finished on the railways because of that. There are so many things to go wrong on the diesels, and they were frightened they wouldn't know how to deal with it.'

And a driver whose working life began at the outbreak of the 1939 war recalled: 'I looked forward to the new techniques and new technology. I knew the hard graft of firing steam engines and the coming of diesel was a challenge. It meant we'd have a cleaner job and more comfortable conditions — no sparks flying, no grime and dust and dirty oil, heavy boots, overalls. Now we were sitting in armchairs with just the press button. But there were a lot of things we lost — pride in the job was lost, I think, because with steam each day was a challenege. You had to give so much to the steam engine in order for it to respond properly. It was like a human being in that sense. Now the diesel doesn't have that at all. Everything is behind you — covered up — you hardly see any moving parts and it's just buttons and switches.

1958-built diesel multiple unit 3-car Suburban Train on the Treherbert — Penarth line working at Porth, 1975. The train is in overall blue livery with yellow ends. Subsequently these trains have been internally refurbished and are in white and blue livery.
(British Railways).

You rely on the mechanism of your locomotive rather than on the skill of the fireman and driver. And there's not the same fellow feeling these days with the diesel as there was with the steam engine.'

The new era began in North Wales with the arrival of two-car diesel sets on the Llandudno-Blaenau Ffestiniog and Bangor-Amlwch services in 1956. In the summer, trains were made up of two sets. Writing in the *Railway World,* Geoffrey Oates remarked that 'good observation at the front end of the train enables passengers to have a footplate view of the track ahead, which can be most fascinating, especially to the railway enthusiast.' He went on: 'Except for the daily goods train from Llandudno Junction to Blaenau Ffestiniog, nothing is seen of the steam engine, nor does the loud echo of the exhaust of labouring trains disturb the peaceful villages through which the route passes . . . The introduction of diesel trains has made it possible for tourists to appreciate the beauty of the countryside to better advantage, although previously an observation coach had been attached to the end of certain steam trains during the summer months.'

In South Wales, diesel multiple units were introduced for local services in 1957 and in September 1961 the steam-hauled Pullmans gave way to Blue Pullman diesel sets. The Blue Pullman set new standards of speed and comfort, leaving Swansea at 6.40 a.m. and arriving in Paddington at 10.15 a.m. after covering the 133 miles from Newport in 127 minutes. The following year, diesel locomotives began running the other main line services.

Technically the Modernisation Plan was a triumph, but it left the railways' basic problems untouched. The huge losses of the late Fifties and early Sixties emphasised that the network was too large and the charges unrealistic. Both the Ministry of Transport and the BTC answered their critics by maintaining that services could not be priced properly because of deficiencies in the accounting system. 'We find one of the most difficult things in the Ministry is to discover where the money is actually being lost,' the Permanent Secretary to the Ministry rather plaintively told a Select Committee in 1960. Some branch lines had been closed since the plan was launched, but management complained that the process of public consultation was too cumbersome and led to delays of two years or more. The time was ripe for an axe, and the man wielding it has passed into railway folklore as a kind of Demon King — Dr Richard Beeching, who was brought in from Imperial Chemical Industries in 1962. He applied the accountant's clinical judgements to Britain's railway system, and the result was not to the liking of those who believed that the usefulness of rail could not be measured solely in terms of profit and loss.

In his Reshaping Report of 1963, he suggested that 400 passenger services should be withdrawn or modified in Britain as a whole and over 2,000 stations and 5,000 route miles of track closed to passenger traffic.

1,700 hp diesel-hydraulic locomotive with Swansea — Manchester train at Margam, 1963. These locomotives, known as 'Hymeks' are no longer in service.
(British Railways).

There was to be selected development of trunk routes and rationalisation of routes between large cities. Freight services were to be overhauled and the liner train introduced for containerised merchandise. The Railways Board — the new managing body after the scrapping of the British Transport Commission by the Tories in the Transport Act of 1962 — thought the proposals 'conservative with regard to closures.' That was not the way they looked in Wales. There were strident protests at the suggestion that 17 passenger services should be withdrawn and no fewer than 190 stations and halts closed. The threatened services included Bangor-Afon Wen and Ruabon-Barmouth in the north, Carmarthen-Aberystwyth in the south-west and Porth-Maerdy and Abercynon-Aberdare in the Valleys. This was in addition to the cuts already proposed, such as the closure of the Central Wales line from Swansea/Llanelli to Shrewsbury and the Carmarthen-Llandeilo line.

Howls of protest rose from public figures and private individuals. What hope was there for Wales if such a ruthless pruning took place? Some of the cries came from enthusiasts for whom the closure of a much-cherished line was felt as a personal injury. Others were inspired by deep-seated fears that a weakened infrastructure would hasten depopulation and militate against attempts to attract industry. The arguments went on for years. One of the lines originally marked down for closure by Beeching — Bridgend-Treherbert via Maesteg and Blaengwynfi — remained open until 1970. Others were spared — or, to use the more popular word, 'reprieved', the language of Death Row giving the right touch of melodrama to an emotive subject. These included the Llandudno-Blaenau Ffestiniog branch line, the Cardiff-Coryton commuter service and the Central Wales, which had a stubborn capacity for survival which sustained it through many a crisis. Forty-five of the 190 stations and halts threatened by Beeching were spared, and one more, Penally, displayed a gift for resurrection by being reopened after closure. Twenty-two of the 70 stations and halts earmarked for closure before Beeching survived, but some evocative names disappeared from the map — Aberdare High Level, Crumlin High Level, Hafodyrynys Platform, Mountain Ash Cardiff Road. It was already too late to save Aberavon Sea Side, Bangor-on-Dee, Moat Lane Junction and a host of others. Their closure, in the official phrase, had 'already been implemented.'

Beeching's case was strongly argued. The Reshaping Report was the first really scientific study of the railway system in the United Kingdom, and it proved that the greater part of it was uneconomic. The figures produced were a crushing retort to the sentimental: one-third of the route mileage carried only one per cent of the freight and passenger traffic, and half of the stations produced only two per cent of passenger receipts. Stopping trains made an overall loss of £66 million in 1961, and the direct costs of operating them were nearly twice the revenue. It was when he looked at the inter-city routes that Beeching's eyes brightened. Their direct costs were amply covered, and the report spoke of the potential for 'fast and semi-fast' services between the major centres of population. 'For people travelling on business who rate their convenience and comfort highly, rail will remain preferable to road transport, provided that continued attention is given to the speed, reliability and comfort of trains.'

'Blue Pullman' on London — Swansea run at Newport, 1967. The train is in its later livery of grey with blue window band and yellow ends.
(British Railways).

Beeching's Pill, as the Press irresistibly called it, was not the perfect remedy. The report was criticised for failing to discuss economies which might have enabled some services to keep going on a reduced basis, and, more importantly, for looking at the railways in isolation. 'Social cost' became a fashionable phrase. In the long run, was it not better business to subsidise an uneconomic suburban line than to close it and increase congestion on the roads? At the very least, the Reshaping Report helped to crystallise attitudes.

In the event, the proposals were not allowed to run their full course. Seven months after the return of a Labour Government in October 1964 Dr Beeching left the Railways Board, and in July 1966 a White Paper rejected commercial viability as the first priority and said the railway system should fit in more closely with the country's economic needs. Nevertheless, the network had substantially diminished. By the end of the year 13,700 route miles were open to traffic, against nearly 17,500 in 1962 and 19,600 in 1948.

For all the furore, it must be remembered that lines were being closed long before Beeching saw the inside of a railway boardroom. If the old companies had not rid themselves of uneconomic services, the system inherited by British Rail would have been scarcely manageable. And the years leading up to his brief but explosive reign had seen many old friends fall by the way-

British Rail's newest and most powerful diesel-electric freight locomotive, the Class 56, took over the operation of the heaviest trains in August 1979.
(British Railways).

side. In 1958, four lines in the Cardiff Division had been closed to passenger traffic — Abergavenny-Merthyr, Bridgend-Nantymoel, Llantrisant-Penygraig and Pantyffynnon-Brynamman West. In 1959 the Chepstow-Monmouth and Ross-on-Wye-Monmouth services bit the dust. Risca-Nantybwch was a casualty in 1960, but the tears of the railway buff that year were reserved for the Mumbles Railway. For the last time those distinctive double-deck electric cars ran smoothly along the shining track beside the sea to end more than a century and a half of railway history. The Oystermouth Railway, as it was originally named, had run the world's first public rail passenger service in 1807, although 70 years passed before horse traction gave way to steam. Its heyday at the turn of the century, when the trains were so packed on bank holidays that passengers determined to make the ride clung perilously outside, gave way to leaner times and the South Wales Tran-

The original horse drawn train of the Oystermouth Railway Company.

"*Off to the Mumbles*"

sport Company, owners in its latter days, decided to close the line when they found they needed £350,000 to keep the trains running.

By 1964 the quiet revolution in British Rail had progressed so far that there were almost as many diesel as steam locomotives — 4,462 against 4,970. And the end of an era came with the last steam-hauled service in South Wales — an early morning train from Gloucester which steamed into Cardiff with a Gloucester-based engine in the first few days of 1966. Two and a half years later the last regular standard gauge British Rail steam service ran out of Preston, and it was time to reflect that in the short space of 13 years nearly 18,500 steam engines had been scrapped or otherwise taken out of service. Some had been built as late as 1960, and there were ex-GWR Castles with years of life in them. Railwaymen shook their heads in wonder. Such things defied logic.

Meanwhile, a new political egg was about to be hatched. It was Barbara Castle's Transport Act of 1968, which for the first time allowed Government grants for unremunerative passenger services to be kept open if the 'social or economic' reasons were strong enough. Sometimes, however, the reasons were more political than either social or economic. In his diaries, Richard Crossman tells of a Cabinet discussion on the future of the Central Wales line in 1969. This was, he said, a 'parody' of a railway, with only 100 passengers in the winter and 200 in the summer. He thought there was 'an overwhelming case for permanent closure next January, because otherwise we will have to pay a £300,000 subsidy.' Transport Minister Richard Marsh argued for closure but, says Crossman, the others started playing politics. According to him, they were in favour of the subsidy 'because three seats were in danger in central Wales.'

The idea of subsidising particular lines went out with the Railways Act of 1974, which gave BR more flexibility in its use of Treasury cash and took the move away from the philosophy of a self-financing railway system a stage further. In future, BR would receive a Public Service Obligation Grant enabling it to maintain a passenger service 'comparable with that provided at the beginning of 1975'. In other words, the taxpayer funded the difference between the amount raised from fares and the cost of running the service — though freight trains had to be self-supporting. Beeching was already beginning to look like ancient history.

In October 1976, another milestone was reached with the introduction of the high-speed train between Paddington and South Wales. This stream-lined Inter-City 125 seemed the last word in rail travel. Passengers marvelled at its speed and comfort. The coaches were double-glazed and air-conditioned. Interior doors opened and closed of their own accord. Friendly voices came over the public address system. The journey time from Cardiff to London was spectacularly reduced from 2 hours 15 minutes to 1 hour 45 minutes, and Swansea to London from 3 hours 20 minutes to 2 hours

Opposite:
Mumbles Railway steam and electric trains. One of the greatest losses in practical and scenic transport in the history of railways in Wales.

45 minutes. Strange to think that, in 1890, the GWR had introduced a new 'fast' service from Cardiff to London — taking a little over four hours . . .

The railwaymen of that time would have been amazed by far more than the speed of trains had they been able to take a peep into the future. Where were the level crossing keepers and signalmen in their high, lonely outposts? Overnight, it seemed, technology had replaced people. Automatic barriers raised and lowered their arms; warning bells shrilled at approaching motorists. At other crossings there were only flashing lights, while some had signalmen maintaining surveillance through closed circuit television. By the late 1970s, vast stretches of track were controlled by central signalling. Thanks to the gadgetry known as continuous track circuiting, three signal boxes — at Newport, Cardiff and Port Talbot — controlled the South Wales main line from the Bristol end of the Severn Tunnel to a point between Llanelli and Pembrey, more than 80 miles to the west.

Some of the old artefacts were disappearing, and others were being reconstructed. In 1979 the old railway bridge at Acrefair, between Ruabon and Llangollen, was demolished. Built in 1860, it was one of the works of Henry Robertson — a Scot who was intended for the ministry but instead became a railway engineer, bringing some of the early lines to North Wales. His great viaduct across the Dee at Cefn-mawr, however, still remained. On the shores of the Menai, work was well advanced at the end of 1979 on the road deck above the railway on the Britannia Bridge, a bold concept which followed the disastrous fire of 1970 which hopelessly buckled Robert Stephenson's wrought iron box girders. The tubular bridge was no more, but the towers and abutments of the original structure were retained to give at least a hint of Stephenson's masterpiece. The new road crossing, linking with the Fishguard-Bangor trunk road on the mainland and the A5 to Holyhead at Llanfair PG in Anglesey, was expected to relieve the congestion on Telford's Menai Bridge just to the east.

Meanwhile, the boffins continued to apply themselves to the problem that had excited the minds of Brunel and Stephenson at the dawn of the Railway Age — how to equate maximum speed with maximum safety. The advanced passenger train, capable of hurtling along at 155 mph, was in the offing. Three of these electric trains were being built for the Euston Glasgow run; the gas turbine experimental APT had already been consigned to the Railway Museum in York.

Such is the pace of railway change. As in every technological field in the 20th century, today's wonder is tomorrow's antique. Steam held sway for more than a century, but as the 1980s dawned the days of diesel already seemed numbered. The BR chairman, Sir Peter Parker, spoke of electrifying the main strategic routes by the turn of the century. Electric locomotives said the experts, were simpler, lighter, cheaper, more durable — and more reliable.

Opposite:
The train of the future: The Advanced Passenger Train developed by scientists and engineers at the Railway Technical Centre, Derby, will enable existing railway lines to be used for 150 mph train services without expensive modification. The picture shows the APT-E demonstrating its body tilting capabilities during the first series of track trials.
(British Railways).

It seemed like the re-run of an old record. And, as the discussion papers piled up on official desks and one theory trod on the heels of another, it was understandable that the steam engine, symbol for so long of railway motive power, kept its hold on the imagination. Its appeal, perhaps, lay in the fact that it wasn't just a machine. It had an animal vigour about it. 'Give me the old iron horse every time,' sighed an old GWR driver, Ivor Evans, at his home in Carmarthen.

It was an odd phrase to use in the 1970s. We could have been back in the time of Trevithick. Man's inventive genius, perhaps, outstrips the scope of his affections.

Acknowledgements

My thanks are due to all those who helped me, either with their encouragement or by providing me with information, in the preparation of this book. I am particularly indebted to Mr Neil Sprinks, Public Relations Officer, South Wales Division, British Rail, and Mr Selwyn James, Assistant Public Relations Officer; Mr Roger Jones, Public Relations Officer, British Rail, Stoke-on-Trent; Mr Alastair Warrington, Senior Technical Officer, British Rail, Newport; Mr Roger Padfield and other members of staff at Cardiff Reference Library; Mr Eric Mountford; Mr E. H. Evans; Mr Ivor M. Morris; Mr R. Lock; Mr J. D. Thorne; Mr Gerald Robinson; Mr Howard Jones; and all those who responded to appeals for information about various aspects of railway history. Mr J. E. Martin kindly provided me with some fine photographs from his personal collections and Mr L. A. Winter of Pronto Photo History and Mr Roy Mason of the Wales Tourist Board were extremely helpful. I must also thank all the railwaymen and ex-railwaymen who went out of their way to assist me, especially Mr Ellis Powell, Mr Myrddin Powell, Mr Edmund Lewis, Mr Mozart Thomas, Mr David Owen and Mr Ivor Evans. The research facilities at the Public Record Office, the British Museum and its associated Newspaper Library, and the National Library of Wales were, as always, invaluable. I am grateful to Mrs Ann Jenkins and Mrs Iona Edwards for their secretarial help and to Mrs Myfanwy Thomas and Messrs Faber & Faber Ltd. for permission to quote from Adlestrop by Edward Thomas. Above all, however, I must thank my wife Dorothy for her enthusiastic support and her help in research and proof-reading.

Reference Sources

Newspapers

Caernarvon Herald; The Cambrian; Cambrian News; Cardiff Times; Carmarthen Journal; Chester Chronicle; Chester Courant; Glamorgan, Monmouth and Brecon Gazette and Merthyr Guardian — later the Cardiff and Merthyr Guardian; Liverpool Daily Post; Monmouthshire Merlin; Montgomeryshire Express; North Wales Chronicle; South Wales Daily News; South Wales Echo; The Times; Welsh Gazette; Western Mail.

Magazines

Great Western Railway Magazine; Herapath's Railway Journal; Illustrated London News; Railway Magazine; Railway News; Railway Times.

Books

E. L. Ahrons: The British Steam Railway Locomotive from 1825 to 1925. Published 1927.
Derek H. Aldcroft: British Railways in Transition. 1968.
Cecil J. Allen: Titled Trains of Great Britain. 1967.
D. S. Barrie:
  The Taff Vale Railway. 1950.
  The Rhymney Railway. 1952.
  The Brecon and Merthyr Railway. 1957.
  The Barry Railway. 1962.
Peter E. Baughan: The Chester and Holyhead Railway. 1972.
Earl of Bessborough: The Diaries of Lady Charlotte Guest. 1950.
Thomas Bevan: Glamorgan Communications. — Article in
  Glamorgan Historian, Vol. 3. 1966.
J. I. C. Boyd:
  Narrow Gauge Lines in Mid Wales. 1965.

Narrow Gauge Lines in South Caernarvonshire. 1971.

The Festiniog Railway. Vol. 1. 1975.

J. E. Campbell, editor: Railway Preservation in North and Mid Wales. 1977.

Ralph Cartwright and R. T. Russell: The Welshpool and Llanfair Light Railway. 1972.

Edgar L. Chappell: History of the Port of Cardiff. 1939.

Rex Christiansen and R. W. Miller: The Cambrian Railways. Vol. 1. 1967; Vol. 2. 1968.

Terry Coleman: The Railway Navvies. 1965.

Lewis Cozens: The Talyllyn Railway. 1948.

Richard Crossman: The Diaries of a Cabinet Minister. 1977.

W. J. K. Davies: Vale of Rheidol Light Railway. 1970.

J. M. Dunn: The Chester and Holyhead Railway. 1968.

Eric Earnshaw: Modern British History for Schools in Wales. 1970.

Hamilton Ellis: British Railway History. 1954.

London Midland and Scottish: A Railway in Retrospect. 1970.

Frank Ferneyhough: The History of Railways in Britain. 1975.

Festiniog Railway Co: A Traveller's Guide to the Festiniog Railway.

C. P. Gasquoine: The Story of The Cambrian. 1922.

Great Western Railway: Brunel and After. 1925.

Great Western Progress, 1935-1935.

Christine Heap and John van Riemsdijk: The Pre-Grouping Railways. 1972.

Geoffrey Kitchenside: Railway Carriage Album. 1966.

British Rail in Action. 1977.

George G. Lerry: Henry Robertson. 1949.

London and North-Western Railway: The Official Illustrated Guide to the London and North-Western Railway. 1859.

E. T. MacDermot, revised by C. R. Clinker: History of the Great Western Railway. Vols. 1. and 2. 1964.

O. S. Nock: Historic Railway Disasters. 1966.

History of the Great Western Railway. Vol. 3. 1967.

The Last Years of British Railways Steam. 1978.

Edward Parry: Parry's Railway Companion from Chester to Holyhead. 1849.

The Railway Executive: British Railways — Today and Tomorrow. 1949.

P. J. G. Ransom: Railways Revived. 1973.

P. Ransome-Wallis: Snowdon Mountain Railway. 1969.

L. T. C. Rolt: Lines of Character. 1952.

Red for Danger. 1955.

Isambard Kingdom Brunel. 1957.

Talyllyn Adventure. 1971.

D. A. Rooksby: Narrow Gauge Railways of Wales. 1973.

Talyllyn Railway Preservation Society: Talyllyn Handbook. 1968.

Margaret Stewart Taylor: The Penydarren Iron Works, 1784-1859 —

Margaret Stewart Taylor: The Penydarren Iron Works, 1784-1859 —
    Article in Glamorgan Historian, Vol. 3. 1966.
Ivor Thomas: Top Sawyer. 1938.
Thomas A. Walker: The Severn Tunnel — Its Construction and Diffi-
culties, 1872-1887 — 1891.
P. B. Whitehouse: Festiniog Railway Revival. 1963.
Charles Wilkins: The History of Merthyr Tydfil. 1908.
John Winton: The Little Wonder: 1975.
H. E. Wright: Welsh Railways. 1975.

Other Sources

Letters, official reports and other documents at the Public Record Office,
London.
Report of the Select Committee on Railway Labourers. 1846.
Taff Vale Railway Rules and Regulations 1853.
Vale of Neath Railway Rules and Regulations 1855.
E. H. Evans: British Railways and the Trade Unions 1825-1975. MS.

Index

A

Aberavon Sea Side, 191.
Abercynon, 11, 17, 190.
Aberdare, 22, 62, 70, 190.
Aberdare High Level, 191.
Aberdare, Lord, *see* Bruce, Henry Austin.
Aberdare Railway, 70.
Aberdare Valley, 73.
Aberdovey, 146.
Aberdylais (Aberdulais), 62.
Aberffrwd, 127.
Abergavenny, 193.
Abergele Disaster, 143, 144 (illus.), 145, 146.
Abergwili, 182.
Abergynolwyn, 116, 118, 119, 174.
Aberllefeni, 118, 119.
Abermule, 148, 149.
Abermule Disaster, 112, 147, 149 (illus.), 150.
Aberthaw, 140.
Aberystwyth, 87, 88, 90-94, 101, 104, 105, 107,
    109, 112, 126-128, 147, 148, 169, 177, 178, 181,
    186, 190.
Aberystwyth & Welsh Coast Railway, 104, 107.
Abt, Dr. Roman, 123.
Accidents: Caerphilly, 73; Cynghordy, 165; Dee
    Bridge, 29, 34 (illus.); Friog 146, Llantrisant,
    146; Newport, 145, 146; Pontypridd, 19, 147;
    Snowdon, 123, 126; South Snowdon, 121; *see
    also* Abergele Disaster, Abermule Disaster,
    Armagh Disaster, and Tay Bridge Disaster.
Acrefair, 197.
Adlestrop, 94.
Advanced Passenger Train, 197 (illus.).
Afon Wen, 120, 190.
Africa, 105.
Alexander Docks, 152.
Alps, 134.
Amalgamated Society of Railway Servants, 109.
Amlwch, 189.
Anglesey, 31, 33, 197.
Archer, Henry, 113, 114.
Armagh Disaster, 148.
Atlas Foundry, 171.

Attlee, Clement, 184.
Aubrey, Sir Thomas, 48.
Auto-Trains, 141.
Awre, 42.

B

Bailey, Crawshay, 13 (illus.), 83.
Bailey, Mrs. Crawshay, 83.
Bala, 181.
Bala, Lake, *see* Llyn Tegid.
Bala Lake Railway, *see* Rheilffordd Llyn Tegid.
Baltimore and Ohio Railway, 153.
Bangor, 26, 30-32, 35, 115, 180, 189, 190, 197.
Bangor-on-Dee, 191.
Bargoed, 72, 77.
Barmouth, 108, 181, 190.
Barnes, George, 181.
Barry, 137, 140.
Barry Island, 140.
Barry Railway, 136-142, 151, 152.
Bartlett, John ('Fighting Barney'), 133.
Bassett-Lowke Company, 183.
Batchelor Brothers, 48.
Batty Menagerie & Circus Band, 83.
Beasley, Ammon, 142.
Beddgelert, 120.
Bedwas, 77.
Beeching, Dr. Richard, 189-192.
Beeching (Reshaping Report), 94, 181, 189-192,
    195.
Benbow, Edward (driver), 92-94.
Berriew, 99.
Berrow, Mrs., 91.
Betws-y-coed, 120.
Beyer Peacock Co., 126.
Birmingham, 108, 156, 158.
Black Rock Hotel, 131.
Blaenau Ffestiniog, 113-115, 177, 181, 189, 190.
Blaengwynfi, 190.
Blakeney, 42.
Blandford, Marquess of, 103.
Blue Pullman, 189, 191 (illus.).

Board of Trade, 78.
Boiler Pool, 92.
Borth, 101, 104, 105.
Boston Lodge, 177.
Boyle, John, 71.
Brean, Thomas, 77.
Brecon, 77, 86, 159.
Brecon Beacons, 77, 159.
Brecon & Merthyr Railway, 74-79, 107, 140, 152, 159, 160.
Breconshire, 85.
Brewer, J. W., 142.
Bridgend, 47, 49, 50, 140, 190, 193.
Bristol, 14, 20, 45, 135.
Bristol Channel, 70.
Bristol & Exeter Railway, 53.
Britannia Bridge, 24, 29-33, 36 (illus.), 39 (illus.), 41, 54, 197.
British Rail, 41, 174, 175, 178, 181, 182, 184, 185, 192, 195, 197.
British Transport Commission, 184, 187, 189, 190.
Briton Ferry, 65.
Broad Gauge, 16, 17, 41, 47, 56, 59, 60, 61, 63, 71, 116, 182.
Bronwydd Arms, 181.
Browne Balfour K.C., 136.
Bruce, Henry Austin (Lord Aberdare), 71.
Brunel, Isambard Kingdom, 13, 14, 16, 30, 32, 40 (illus.), 41, 42, 47-49, 53-55, 59, 61, 62, 64, 65, 185, 197.
Brunel, Sir Marc Isambard, 14, 54.
Brymbo, 33.
Brynaman West, 193.
Bryn Eglwys Quarry, 118.
Bryngwyn, 120.
Bucknell, 81.
Builth Road, 80, 86.
Builth Wells, 81.
Burke (Station-master), 105.
Burns, Robbie, 72.
Burry Port, 151.
Bute, Marquess of, 71, 137.
Bute Trustees, 71, 136, 137, 152.

C

Cader Idris, 117, 119, 120.
Caerberllan Castle, 117.
Cadoxton, 137.
Caerleon, 42.
Caernarfon, 31, 32, 113, 120.
Caernarvonshire, 33, 35.
Caernarvonshire County Council, 121.
Caerphilly, 71, 72, 140, 153.
Caerphilly Mountain, 73.
Caersws, 92, 103.
Caldicot, 131.
Cambrian Coast, 107.
Cambrian Coast Express, 186.
Cambrian News, 91, 120, 127, 128, 146.

Cambrian Railways, 86, 91, 92, 95, 98, 104, 105, 107-109, 112, 118, 119, 126, 146, 148, 151, 152, 178.
Canada, 129.
Capitals United, 156 (illus.), 186.
Cardiff, 11, 13, 14-17, 19, 20, 22, 45-49, 51, 59, 71-73, 74, 108, 135, 136, 137, 153, 156-159, 188, 190, 195, 197.
Cardiff Railway, 152.
Cardigan Bay, 104.
Cardiganshire, 58, 88, 107.
Carmarthen, 49, 58, 80, 86, 87, 94, 163, 168, 169, 182, 190, 198.
Carmarthen and Cardigan Railway, 182.
Carmarthen Journal, 58.
Carmarthen Junction, 169.
Carmarthenshire, 44, 83, 85.
Carno, 105.
Castle, Barbara, 178, 195.
Central Electricity Board, 177.
Central Wales Line, 151, 163-165, 168, 185, 190, 195.
Central Wales Extension Railway, 83.
Central Wales Railway, 80-83, 85-87.
Chancery, 91.
Chattenden and Upnor Railway, 179.
Chepstow, 41, 44, 45, 49-51, 54, 129, 131, 159, 193.
Chepstow Bridge, 54, 55 (illus.).
Chester, 24, 26, 29, 35, 38, 39, 71, 80.
Chester and Holyhead Railway, 24, 26-31, 35, 38.
Chester Chronicle, 33, 35.
Chester Courant, 29.
Christian Malford, 41.
Churchill, Winston, 184.
Clark, Edwin, 33.
Clements (driver), 77.
Coalbrooke Dale Iron Co., 33.
Coles, John (driver), 74.
'College By The Sea', 107.
Conwy, 29.
Conwy Bridge, 24, 29, 30, 32.
Conwy, River, 24.
Cork, 35, 59.
Corris Railway, 101, 119, 120 (illus.), 121 (illus.), 128, 174.
Corwen, 120.
Coryton, 190.
Cowbridge, 49.
Creigiau, 142.
Craven Arms, 81-83, 86.
Crawshay, Richard, 11.
Crawshay Works, 11, 73.
Crewe, 80, 83, 88.
Crossman, Richard, 195.
Crosswood Park, 89.
Crumlin High Level, 191.
Crumlin Viaduct, 65, 66, 68 (illus.).
Cwmbargoed, 74.

D

Dandy Wagons, 114.
Dartmoor, 53.
Davidson & Oughterson, 100.
Davies, David, 88, 89 (illus.), 95, 96, 97 (illus.), 98-102 (illus.), 103, 136, 186.
Davies, Lt.-Col. David, 112.
Davies, William (driver), 146.
Davies and Metcalfe, 127.
Dduallt, 177.
Dee, River, 197.
Dee Bridge, 29.
Denbigh, 98.
Denbighshire, 96.
Denny, Henry, 58.
Derby, 197.
Devil's Bridge, 126-128, 177, 180.
Diarhoea Mixture, 142.
Didcot, 156, 188.
Dinas, Caerns., 120.
Dinas, Rhondda, 21.
Dinas Powis, 142.
Dinorwic Quarries, 179-181.
Dolau, 81.
Dolgellau, 112 (illus.), 147.
Dover, 131.
Dovey, River, 103, 107, 108, 118.
Dovey Junction, 107.
Dowlais, 74.
Dowlais Works, 14, 73.
Drope, 142.
Dublin, 24, 35, 38.
Dudley Zoo, 183.
Dun Laoghaire, 38.
Dunn, Bill (driver), 141.

E

Eastern Region, 174, 175, 177.
Ebbw Valley, 66.
Edwards, Edward, 91.
Egypt, 129.
Elan Valley, 127.
Ellesmere, 105, 107, 109.
Ely, River, 47.
England, George, 114, 177.
Euston, 38, 80, 86, 186, 197.
Evangelization Society, 131.
Evans, David (ganger), 103.
Evans, Ivor (driver), 198.

F

Fairbairn, William, 30.
Fairbourne Railway, 122, 183 (illus.).
Fairlie Locomotives, 116, 117 (illus.), 177 (illus.).
Fairlie, Robert, 115, 116.
Farnham, Lord and Lady, 145.

F

Fenton, Murray & Jackson, 59.
Ferryside, 86.
Festiniog Railway, 111, 113, 114-117, 120, 128, 172 (illus.), 174, 177.
Festiniog Railway Society, 175.
Festiniog Railway Trust, 175.
Ffestiniog, 114, 118.
Fisher, George, 21, 70.
Fishguard, 41, 42, 86, 197.
Fishguard Express, 152 (illus.).
Fletcher, Jennings & Co., 117.
Fleuss diving gear, 130.
Forden, 101.
France, 148.

G

G. & S. Company, 183.
Garraway, Allan, 174, 177.
Garw Valley, 140.
Gladstone's Act 1844, 50.
Glamorgan, 47, 70, 83.
Glamorganshire Canal, 14, 20.
Glansevern, 99, 101.
Glasgow, 197.
Gloucester, 42, 47, 59, 156, 159, 195.
Gloucester & Dean Forest Railway, 42.
Glynneath, 62, 65.
Godfrey, John A., 61.
Gooch, Daniel, 59 (illus.).
Grange Court, 42.
'Great Little Trains of Wales', 113, 171, 183.
Great Western Progress, 160.
Great Western Railway, 14, 16, 41, 42, 58, 59, 64, 65, 73, 74, 77, 86, 90-95, 104, 107, 112, 126, 129, 131, 134, 136, 140, 141, 142, 151-154, 156, 157, 159, 160, 168, 170, 178, 179, 181, 185, 186, 195, 197, 198.
Great Western Railway Magazine, 73.
Guest, Josiah John, 13, 14, 21 (illus.), 76.
Guest, Lady Charlotte, 13, 15, 17, 19.
Gwendraeth Valley, 151.
Gwili Railway, 181, 182.

H

Hafodyrynys Platform, 191.
Harlech, 146.
Hatcham Ironworks, 114.
Haverfordwest, 58, 156.
Hawkshaw, Sir John, 129.
Herapath, George, 26.
Herapath's Railway Journal, 82.
Hengoed, 70, 72.
Hereford, 70, 71, 81, 82.
Hill, Anthony, 14.
Hill, Richard, 11.
Hirwaun, 62.
Holland, Samuel, 113, 114.

Holyhead, 24, 26, 28, 34, 35, 38, 39, 80, 144, 151, 186, 197.
Holyhead Mail, 143.
Holmes (driver), 144.
Home Guard, 168.
Homfray, Samuel, 11.
Hong Kong, 94.
Hood, John, 109.
Hopkinstown, 147.
Horlock Messrs. 179.
Hrone, Sir Robert, 154, 156, 159.
Howell, David, 101.
Hunslet, 180-181.

I

Illustrated London News, 58.
Imperial Chemical Industries, 189.
Imperial Russian Commission, 116.
Inter-City 125, 41, 187 (illus.), 195.
Ireland, 24, 41, 108, 144.
Irish Mail, 38, 186.

J

James, Christopher, 50.
Jones, Dr. Edward, 146.
Jones, Sir Haydn, 171, 173.
Jones, Dr. Hugh, 146.
Jones, Margaret, 95.
Jones, Richard (driver), 91, 92.
Jones, Tom, 181.
Jones, Tom ('Poopsie'), 165.

K

Kennard, T. W., 65.
Kidwelly, 86.
Killarney, 35.
Kilvert, Francis, 41.
Kingstown, 38.
Knight, Rev. Robert, 49.
Knighton, 81, 82, 85, 86.
Knighton Railway, 81, 83.

L

Lambert (diver), 130.
Lampeter, 88, 92-94, 182.
Lancashire, 20, 71, 88.
Lancashire & Carlisle Railway, 39.
Landore, 58.
Landore Viaduct, 44, 52.
Leeds, 71.
Lein Fach, see Vale of Rheidol Railway.
Lewes, Major Price, 128.
Lewis, Daniel, 19.

Lewis, Edmund (driver), 159, 162.
Lisburne, Earl of, 89.
Liverpool, 31, 71, 83, 88, 108, 135.
Liverpool & Manchester Railway, 13.
Liverpool & North Eastern Railway, 151, 159.
Liverpool Daily Post, 145.
Llanberis, 123, 126, 179, 180.
Llanberis Lake Railway, 179, 181.
Llancaiach, 21.
Llanddulais, 143, 145.
Llandeilo, 83, 86, 190.
Llandinam, 88, 95, 96, 99.
Llandovery, 81-83, 85, 86, 164, 165.
Llandrindod Wells, 80-83, 85, 86.
Llandudno, 24, 189, 190.
Llandudno Junction, 189.
Llandyssul, 156.
Llanelli, 58, 83, 86, 90, 185, 190, 197.
Llanelly Railway, 83.
Llanfair Caereinion, 126.
Llanfair P.G., 197.
Llanfihangel, 117.
Llangollen, 197.
Llangurig, 88.
Llanidloes, 86, 88, 91, 95, 98-101, 107.
Llanidloes & Newtown Railway, 95, 96, 98-101, 107.
Llanilar, 92, 94.
Llanpumsaint, 182.
Llansamlet, 53, 54.
Llantrisant, 193.
Llantwit Major, 140.
Llanuwchllyn, 181.
Llanwrtyd Wells, 83, 85, 86, 165.
Llanybyther, 92, 93.
Lleyn Peninsula, 24.
Lloyd George, 151.
Llwyngwril, 107, 146.
Llyn Cwellyn, 121.
Llyn Padarn, 181.
Llyn Tegid, 181.
Llyn Ystradau, 177.
Llynfi Valley, 140.
Locomotives:
  Aberystwyth, 90;
  Acheron, 59;
  Alexander, 59;
  Anglesea, 39;
  Atlas, 78;
  Bellepheron, 59;
  Blanche, 172 (illus.);
  Cader Idris, 77 (illus.), 90;
  Caerphilly Castle, 56 (illus.), 153;
  Caliban, 59;
  Cambrian, 33, 39;
  Cardiff, 21;
  Carmarthen, 92;
  Charon, 59;
  Conway, 39;
  The Countess, 124 (illus.), 126, 179;
  Countess Vane, 103;
  Count Louis, 183;

Denbigh Castle, 155 (illus.);
Dinas, 21;
Dolbadarn, 181;
Dolgoch, 117, 171, 173, 174;
The Dove, 47;
Dowlais, 21;
Duffryn, 22;
The Earl, 126, 179;
Edward Thomas, 174;
Edward VII, 127;
Elidir (Red Damsel), 181;
Enid, 183;
Ernest W. Twining, 183;
Fire Queen, 179;
Gadlys, 22;
General Wood, 90;
Glendower, 39;
Gorgon, 59;
Hecate, 59;
Hector, 59;
Hercules, 74 (illus.);
Hydra, 59;
Katie, 183;
King George V, 153, 160 (illus.);
Ladas, 123;
Lady Elizabeth, 90, 93 (illus.);
Little Giant, 115, 116 (illus.);
Little Wonder, 115 (illus.), 122;
Llancaiach, 21;
Llewellyn, 39, 178;
Lord of The Isles, 56 (illus.);
Maid Marian, 181;
Medusa, 59;
Meirionydd, 176;
Menai, 39;
Merddin Emrys, 117 (illus.), 177;
Merthyr, 21;
Milford, 99;
Moel Siabod, 183;
Montgomery, 92;
Mountaineer, 105 (illus.);
Myrddin/Merlin, 182;
Newbridge, 22 (illus.);
North Star, 56 (illus.);
Owain Glyndwr, 178;
Pegasus, 33;
Penmaenmawr, 39;
Phantom, The, 47;
Phlegethon, 59;
Plymouth, 21;
Plynlimon, 90;
Powis, 39;
Prince, 177;
Prince Edward of Wales, 122;
Prince of Wales, 39, 127, 178;
Rheidor, 127 (illus.);
Rhondda, 21, 22;
Rising Star, 163 (illus.);
Rocket, 186;
St. David, 33, 39;
Severn, 78;
Siân, 183;

Sir Haydn, 174;
Snowdon, 39, 183;
Taff, 21, 22;
Talerddig, 103;
Talyllyn, 117, 171;
Trafalgar, 59;
Victor Emanuel, 59;
Welsh Pony, 115;
Wild Aster, 181;
Wyddfa, 123 (illus.), 183;
Wynnstay, 107 (illus.).
London, 14, 24, 30, 35, 38, 51, 58, 59, 61, 81, 86, 101, 103, 127, 157, 186, 187, 191, 195, 197.
London and North Western Railway, 21, 38, 39, 73, 80, 83, 86, 90, 96, 120, 151, 152, 163.
London Bridge, 127.
London, Midland & Scottish Railway, 39, 151, 152, 159, 163, 185.
London Midland Region, 178, 185.
London Underground, 185.
Lundie, Cornelius, 72, 73.

M

Machynlleth, 101, 103, 104, 107, 118-120, 146.
Machynlleth Station, 110 (illus.).
Maddocks, Williams, 113.
Maerdy, 190.
Maesteg, 190.
Maesycrugiau, 92.
Manchester, 21, 71, 80, 81, 83, 87, 96, 108, 135, 148, 190.
Manchester & Milford Railway, 77, 87-93, 96, 126, 127.
Margam Park, 47.
Marsh, Richard, 195.
Mawddach Estuary, 108, 222.
McDougall, Sir Arthur, 122.
Mead's House, 47.
Menai Strait, 24-26, 30-33, 179, 197.
Menai Bridge, 26, 34, 197.
Merioneth, 96, 114, 147.
Merioneth County Council, 181.
Merthyr Guardian, 14, 16, 17, 20, 45, 47, 49, 50.
Merthyr Tredegar & Abergavenny Railway, 73.
Merthyr Tydfil, 11, 13, 14, 16, 20, 22, 58, 61, 62, 65, 70, 73, 112, 161, 162, 193.
Merthyr Vale Colliery, 73.
Mexico, 116.
Middle Dyffryn, 70.
Middleton Colliery, 123.
Midland Railway, 152.
Mid-Wales Railway, 81, 91, 100.
Milford Haven, 58, 59, 82, 87, 88, 96, 99.
Minffordd, 177.
Moat Lane, 149, 191.
Modernisation Plan 1955, 187, 189.
Mold, 39.
Monachlog Fawr, 90.
Moon, Richard, 83.
Moorson, Captain Richard, 26, 27 (illus.), 28.

Monmouth, 42, 193.
Monmouthshire, 42, 47, 50, 130, 140.
Monmouthshire Merlin, 54, 65, 71.
Monmouthshire Railway, 70.
Montgomery, 149, 150.
Montgomery Express, 150.
Montgomeryshire, 87, 95, 96.
Montgomery Station, 110 (illus.).
Mountain Ash (Cardiff Road), 191.
Mount Rigi, 123.
Mount Washington, 123.
Mumbles, 86.
Mumbles Railway, 193.

N

Nantgarw cutting, 71.
Nantgarw Gap, 140.
Nantlle Railway, 113.
Nantybwch, 73, 193.
Nantymoel, 193.
Navigation (Abercynon), 11, 17, 20.
Neath, 47, 50, 62, 70.
Neath & Brecon Railway, 79, 152.
Nefyn, 24.
Nelson, 21.
Nelson, Lord, 88.
Newbridge, see Pontypridd.
Newcastle, 159.
Newell, Richard (guard), 146.
New Hampshire, 123.
New Passage Ferry, 135.
Newport, 16, 42, 44, 50, 59, 77, 146, 152, 156, 186,
    187, 189, 191, 197.
Newport, Abergavenny & Hereford Railway, 67,
    70.
Newport Corporation, 140.
Newton-Le-Willows, 39.
Newtown, 91, 95, 96, 98-101, 103, 105, 107, 148-
    150.
Newtown & Machynlleth Railway, 101, 107.
New Quay, 156.
New York Herald Tribune, 153.
New Zealand, 116.
Neyland, 42, 58, 88.
Nixon, John, 71, 73.
Norman, James, 77.
Northampton, 61, 183.
North Eastern Region, 185.
North Wales Chronicle, 30, 31.
North Wales Narrow Gauge Railway, 120.

O

Oates, Geoffrey, 189.
Ocean combine, 95, 104, 136.
Ogmore, 137.
Ogmore Valley, 140.
Ormeshead (Llandudno), 24.
Oswestry, 96, 98, 100, 101, 105, 107, 120.

Oswestry, Ellesmere & Whitchurch Railway, 107.
Oswestry & Newtown Railway, 101, 105, 107.
Overend and Gurney Bank, 88, 108.
Owen, Mrs. Anne, 99, 101.
Owen, David (driver), 163.
Owen, John (fireman), 148.
Oystermouth Railway, 193.

P

Padarn Country Park, 181.
Padarn Railway, 179, 180.
Paddington, 41, 59, 156, 186, 189, 195.
Pantyffynnon, 193.
Parker, Sir Peter, 197.
Parry, Edward, 24.
Peckett & Sons, 182.
Pegler, Alan, 175.
Pembrey, 197.
Pembroke, 50.
Pembrokeshire, 44, 58, 80.
Pembroke Dock, 80.
Pembroke Coast Express, 154 (illus.), 186.
Penallta, 73.
Penally, 191.
Penarth, 47, 188.
Pencader, 87, 88, 92, 93, 96, 127.
Pengam, 72.
Penmaenmawr, 28.
Penmon, 31.
Penrhyn Castle, 180.
Penrhyn point, 122.
Penrhyndeudraeth, 177.
Penstrowed, 96.
Penydarren Tramroad, 11.
Penydarren works, 13.
Penygraig, 193.
Perkins, T. R., 90.
Perrett, Jack, 142.
Pethick Brothers, 127.
Piercy, Benjamin, 101 'illus.).
Plas Madoc, 96.
Plymouth, 127.
Plymouth, Earl of, see Windsor, Lord.
Plymouth Works, 11, 14.
Pole, Sir Felix, 153, 160.
Pontardulais, 83, 86.
Pontypool, 70.
Pontypool Road, 70, 146.
Pontypridd, 14, 19, 20, 137, 147.
Port Dinorwic, 179.
Porth, 188, 190.
Porthdynllaen, 24, 101, 108.
Porthkerry Park, 140.
Porthmadog, 108, 113, 114, 120, 121, 147, 174,
    177.
Portskewett, 129, 135.
Port Talbot, 50, 186, 197.
Powell, Ellis (driver), 168, 169.
Powell, Thomas, 70.
Preston, 195.

Pringle, Col., 150.
Pritchard, Thomas, 114.
Prytherch, Ianto, 165.
Public Record Office, 61.
Public Service Obligation Grant, 195.
Pumlumon, 101.
Punch Magazine, 60, 159.
Pwllheli, 108, 112, 120.

Q

Quakers Yard, 19, 70, 73, 161.
Queen Victoria, 14, 36, 108.
Quellyn, 121.

R

Radnor Forest, 81.
Radnorshire, 81.
Radnorshire Rifle Volunteers, 82.
Railcars, 141, 158 (illus.).
Railway Adventure, 174.
Railway Executive Committee, 185, 186.
Railway Magazine, 85, 90.
Railway Mania, 47, 88.
Railway Museum, York, 197.
Railway Technical Centre, 197.
Railway Times, 15, 54, 65, 67.
Railway World, 189.
Railways Act 1921, 136, 159.
Railways Act 1974, 195.
Railways Board, 190, 192.
Red Dragon, 162 (illus.), 186.
Rendell, J. K., 90, 91.
Resolven, 62, 165.
Rhayader, 100.
Rheidol Mines, 127.
Rheidol Valley, 126, 127.
Rheilffordd Llyn Padarn, *see* Llanberis Lake Railway.
Rheilffordd Llyn Tedig, 181.
Rheilffordd Gwili, *see* Gwili Railway.
Rhondda, 22, 70, 104, 136, 137, 142, 147.
Rhyd-ddu, 120, 121.
Rhydycar, 162.
Rhydyronen, 174.
Rhyl, 98.
Rhymney, 70, 73.
Rhymney Bridge, 74.
Rhymney, River, 47, 72, 140,
Rhymney Railway, 70, 71, 73, 74, 77, 137, 140, 142, 151-153.
Rhymney Valley, 72.
Rich, Col., 145.
Richards, Richard, 115.
Riggenbach, Niklaus, 123.
Risca, 193.
Rising Sun Deviation, 77.
Ritson, W., 65.
Roath Basin Junction, 73.

Roberts, William, 146.
Robertson, Henry, 197.
Rolfe, Charles, 33.
Rolt, L. T. C., 171, 173, 174, 175 (illus.).
Romiley, 127.
Ross-on-Wye, 193.
Rotherhithe, 54.
Ruabon, 96, 181, 190, 197.
Rumney Tramroad, 77.
Rumcord, 31.
Russell, Charles, 47.
Russell, J. C., 90, 91.
Russell, Jim, 171.
Russia, 129.
Ruston Engine, 181.
Ryan, C. N., 85, 86.

S

Salisbury, 85.
Saltney, 29.
Saunders, Charles, 62.
Saunders, Frederick, 62.
Savin, Thomas, 95, 98 (illus.), 99-101, 104, 105, 107, 108.
Savoy Hotel, 162.
Scafell cutting, 99.
Scandinavia, 141.
Scotland, 19, 168.
Scott, Sir Walter, 73.
Select Committee on Railway Labourers, 26.
Seven Mile Bank, 78.
Severn Bridge, 48 (illus.), 135.
Severn Lamb Company, 181.
Severn, River, 42, 103, 129.
Severn Tunnel, 42, 129-134 (illus.), 135, 136, 142, 159, 197.
Sharp, Roberts & Co., 21.
Sharp, Stewart & Co., 78, 93, 104, 105, 141.
Sheffield, 108.
Shrewsbury, 80-83, 85-87, 104, 105, 171, 178, 185, 190.
Shropshire, 81, 107.
Smiles, Samuel, 28.
Smith, Montague, 127.
Snowdonia, 88.
Snowdon Mountain Railway, 123, 126, 179 (illus.), 183.
Snowdon Ranger, 121.
South Devon Railway, 53, 62.
Southern Railway, 151.
Southern Region, 185.
South Snowdon, 121.
South Wales Daily News, 60, 134, 135.
South Wales Railway, 41-43, 48, 49, 58, 59, 61, 62, 65.
South Wales Transport Co., 193, 195.
Spooner, Charles, 114.
Spooner, James, 113, 114, 117.
Spooner, James Swinton, 117.
Stephenson, George, 24, 26, 30, 186.

Stephenson, Robert, 24, 28-32 (illus.), 33, 34, 39, 41, 42, 114, 197.
Stockport, 127.
Stockton and Darlington Railway, 13, 21.
Stowbridge, 183.
Strata Florida, 88-90, 94.
St. David's, 156.
St. Fagans, 45.
St. Georges, 142.
Stuck, Thomas, 62.
Sudan, The, 129.
Sudbrook, 131-133.
Sugar Loaf Line, *see* Central Wales Line.
Sugar Loaf Mountain, 83, 85 (illus.), 165.
Sully, 142.
Swansea, 12, 41, 44, 45, 49-51, 58, 59, 65, 80-86, 91, 159, 168, 185, 186, 189-191, 195.
Swindon, 59, 62, 92, 160, 174.
Swiss Locomotive & Machine Works, 183.
Switzerland, 123, 183.
Szlummer, Sir James, 127, 137.

T

Taff Bargoed Railway, 73.
Taff, River, 47.
Taff Vale, 20.
Taff Vale Railway, 14-19 (illus.), 20-24, 50, 61, 64, 70, 71, 73, 136, 137, 140, 142, 146, 151, 152.
Taffs Well, 70, 140.
Talbot, C. R. M., 47.
Talbot, Joseph, 131.
Talybont, 78, 79.
Talybont Bank, 159.
Talerddig cutting, 101, 102 (illus.), 103.
Talyllyn Lake, 117, 120.
Talyllyn Railway, 116-120, 171, 173-175.
Talyllyn Railway Preservation Soc., 173.
Tank Pool, *see* Boiler pool.
Tan-y-Bwlch, 117, 172 (illus.), 174, 177.
Tanygrisiau, 177.
Tawe, River, 52.
Tay Bridge Disaster, 146.
Tayleur, Chas & Co., 39.
Teify, River, 92.
Teify Valley Preservation Society, 181.
Telford, Thomas, 14, 25 (illus.), 26, 34, 197.
Tenby, 80.
The Little Wonder (book), 177.
Thomas, Edward, 173.
Thomas, Edward (poet), 94.
Thomas, John (driver), 74.
Thomas, Mozart (driver), 164.
Thomas, Will (driver), 77.
Thomas, William (guard), 77.
Thompson, Francis, 29, 30.
Tidenham, 47.
Times, The, 143, 145, 173.
Tir Phil, 72.
Tondu, 140.
Torpantau, 77, 78, 162.

Town Missionary and Scripture Readers Society, 26.
Towy Valley, 86.
Towyn, 101, 116, 118, 119, 171, 173, 174.
Towyn Wharf, 173.
Transport Act 1953, 186.
Transport Act 1962, 190.
Transport Act 1968, 195.
Transport Bill, 171.
Transport, Minister of, 178.
Transport, Ministry of, 189.
Trawscoed, 89, 92, 94.
Trawsfynydd Station, 111 (illus.).
Tredegar Park, 146.
Treforest, 137.
Tregaron, 88, 94.
Tregaron Bog, 88, 94.
Trehafod, 137.
Treherbert, 188, 190.
Trelewis Colliery, 161.
Tremadoc, 113.
Trevithick, Richard, 11, 12 (illus.), 13, 198.
Trinder, Bill, 171, 173.
Tryfan Junction, 120.
Tunnels:
  Caerphilly, 73;
  Llwyncoch, 81;
  Mersey, 134;
  Merthyr, 65;
  Newport, 44;
  Pencaedrain, 62, 65;
  Penmaenbach, 29;
  Penmaenmawr, 28;
  Penybont, 81;
  Quakers Yard, 19;
  Sugar Loaf, 83, 84 (illus.), 85 (illus.), 164;
  Thames, 13, 14;
  Torpantau, 77; *see also* Severn Tunnel.
Twynshon Evan Curve, 77.
Tyer's Electric Tablet, 148.
Tythegstone Court, 49.

U

United States of America, 88, 153.
University of Wales, 107.
Usk, River, 44.
Usk Valley, 42.

V

Vacuum Brake, 92.
Vale of Clwyd Line, 98.
Vale of Glamorgan, 48.
Vale of Glamorgan Railway, 140.
Vale of Neath Railway, 61, 63-67, 70.
Vale of Rheidol Railway, 126-128, 177, 1 (illus.).
Vale of Towy Railway, 83, 86.
Vauxhall Bridge, 127.

Viaducts: Barmouth, 108; Cefn Coed, 77, 78 (illus.); Cefn Mawr, 197; Cyngordy, 82-84 (illus.), 85, 165; Dolgoch, 117; Ffestiniog, 118 (illus.); Knucklas, 81; Llanbradach, 140; Newport, 44; Pont Aberbargoed, 71; Pont-lottyn, 71; Pontsarn, 77; Pontypridd, 14; Porth-kerry, 140; Quakers Yard, 19; Walnut Tree, 140; *see also* Crumlin Viaduct and Landore Viaduct.

W

Walker, Thomas, 129-135.
Walnut Tree, 70-72.
Warrens Patent, 67.
Warwickshire, 71.
Waterloo Day, 49.
Waterford, 58.
Watford, 86.
Watt, James, 186.
Welsh Gazette, 91, 92.
Welsh Highland Railway, 121, 122 (illus.), 175.
Welsh Marches, 104.
Welshpool, 109, 126.
Welshpool and Llanfair Railway, 124, 126, 179, 182 (illus.).
Wenvoe, 137.
Westbury on Severn, 42.
Western Mail, 19, 137, 145, 146, 184.

Western Region, 185.
Walley, George Hammond, 95, 96, 99, 100.
Whitchurch, 105, 107, 120, 148, 149.
Whitehaven, 117.
Wild Runs, 78.
Wilkins, Charles, 14.
Williams, Glyn, 181.
Williams, William (driver), 74.
Wiltshire, 41.
Winterthur, 183.
Winton, John, 177.
Wye, River, 54.
Wynn, Colonel, 100.
Wynn, Watkin Williams, 100.
Wynne, Ald. E. P., 128.

Y

Ynyslas, 104, 107, 108.
York, 197.
Yorkshire, 71, 123.
Ystradmeurig, 89, 90.
Ystrad Mynach, 72, 73.

Z

Zillertalbahn, 179.